*How to Make
Your Care Home Fun*

of related interest

Involving Families in Care Homes
A Relationship-Centred Approach to Dementia Care
Bob Woods, John Keady and Diane Seddon
ISBN 978 1 84310 229 8
Bradford Dementia Group Good Practice Guides

The Creative Arts in Palliative Care
Edited by Nigel Hartley and Malcolm Payne
ISBN 978 1 84310 591 6

Design for Nature in Dementia Care
Garuth Chalfont
ISBN 978 1 84310 571 8
Bradford Dementia Group Good Practice Guides

The Pool Activity Level (PAL) Instrument for Occupational Profiling
A Practical Resource for Carers of People with Cognitive Impairment
Third Edition
Jackie Pool
ISBN 978 1 84310 594 7
Bradford Dementia Group Good Practice Guides

Remembering Yesterday, Caring Today
Reminiscence in Dementia Care: A Guide to Good Practice
Pam Schweitzer and Errollyn Bruce
Foreword by Faith Gibson
ISBN 978 1 84310 649 4
Bradford Dementia Group Good Practice Guides

Reminiscence Theatre
Making Theatre from Memories
Pam Schweitzer
Foreword by Glenda Jackson MP
ISBN 978 1 84310 430 8

Ageing, Disability and Spirituality
Addressing the Challenge of Disability in Later Life
Edited by Elizabeth MacKinlay
ISBN 978 1 84310 584 8

How to Make Your Care Home Fun

Simple Activities for People of All Abilities

KENNETH AGAR

Jessica Kingsley Publishers
London and Philadelphia

The author and publishers are grateful to the proprietor below for permission to quote the following material: Extract from 'It Was Long Ago' by E. Farjeon. From *Blackbird Has Spoken* by E. Farjeon (1999). Reprinted by permission of David Higham Associates.

First published in 2009
by Jessica Kingsley Publishers
116 Pentonville Road
London N1 9JB, UK
and
400 Market Street, Suite 400
Philadelphia, PA 19106, USA

www.jkp.com

Library of Congress Cataloging in Publication Data

Agar, Kenneth.
How to make your care home fun : simple activities for people of all abilities / Kenneth Agar.
p. cm.
ISBN 978-1-84310-952-5 (pb : alk. paper)
1. Nursing homes--Recreational activities. 2. Older people--Recreation. I. Title.
RA999.R42A43 2009
362.16--dc22

2008024248

British Library Cataloguing in Publication Data
A CIP catalogue record for this book is available from the British Library

ISBN 978 1 84310 952 5

Printed and bound in Great Britain by
Athenaeum Press, Gateshead, Tyne and Wear

I undertook the editing
of this book with my daughter,
geriatrician Dr Katherine Wright,
when my father, Kenneth Agar,
died in 2006.
It is dedicated to the memory
of my mother Daphne Agar,
who died of Alzheimer's.

Sue Rolfe

Kenneth Agar was chairman of the Exmouth Alzheimer's Society for 13 years until his death in December 2006. During that time he campaigned actively to improve the care and welfare of those suffering from the disease. He organised many activities for local groups, including outings and regular tea dances. He also worked for some years as a lay inspector for care homes in Devon for the local authority. What he witnessed inspired him to write this book. Running through it, however, is also a lifetime of creativity based on his work as a poet and writer of education school books. He was headmaster of Newham Primary School before he retired to Devon in 1978.

Contents

Foreword

In our care homes for older people live some of the most interesting and wisest people you could ever hope to meet. They are a tremendous mix of personalities, abilities and interests, coming from a rich variety of social and cultural backgrounds. For various reasons they have reached a stage when they need to live in a care home where care staff can help them to meet their needs. At long last there is growing recognition that these needs consist of more than just physical care, and that we all need to be engaged in activities from time to time that enable us to meet our social, psychological, creative and cultural needs. It is through these activities that we find meaning in life and we express who we are to the world. This may be particularly important for people who have had to leave their own home to move into a care home.

Kenneth Agar's book makes a very strong case for activity programmes in care homes. It describes in helpful detail how activity organisers can develop a myriad of different kinds of creative, interesting and participatory activities for the residents in their care. Offering variety and choice is the stimulus to finding the right activity for each individual. These activities are the best way to provide person-centred care for people with many needs and with many assets.

Person Centred Care means listening to people to find out what is most important to them. Assumptions are not made. Care is holistic and centres on the whole person: who they are, their life before, and how they currently feel. Care planning and assessment include the strengths, abilities and preferences of the individual. The emphasis is on what they *can* do, rather than what they cannot do. ('Listen to What I'm Saying', a DVD by Age Exchange)

We heartily recommend this book to everyone with an interest in care homes for older people. We want to work towards a society in which every community knows about and is proud of its local care homes for older people. This book has a big part to play in making this happen.

Bernie Arigho and David Savill
Age Exchange

1

Introduction

What do they do all day?

This book examines the need for, and offers a practical programme of, activities for older people in nursing and residential homes, day centres, rehabilitation centres and hospices. Even at home.

Why 'activities'? If the word suggests energetic action, being very busy, or entering wheelchair races, that is not the intention. Activities can mean everyday occupations, interests, hobbies, pastimes, and all the myriad of things that older people might have been undertaking in the past.

This book is about how the residents in care homes for older people might spend their time. It will:

- examine how care homes are run, how they are regulated in the light of recent legislation, and how they are inspected

- consider what services are provided by care homes and what is lacking

- provide a selection of activities and occupations that have proved successful with elderly people in current care homes.

Why is a book like this necessary?

Here are some frequently heard comments made by relatives, friends and other visitors of residents in care homes:

- 'They never seem to be doing anything.'
- 'Most of them just sit and go to sleep.'
- 'What do they do all day?'

There are some care homes that provide exceptions to these views, but sadly they are in a minority. The over-riding impression of most care homes is one of depressing inertia. How has this come about? Largely through the institutional-ised practices of the past, and the ageism of present times. There is also a low expectation of what older people in care homes can still do.

This book shows you how this situation can be changed through creative programming and 'activity nursing'.

2

The Care Homes Sector

In 2008 there were over 449,648 care home places in 18,527 care homes in England. Health care professionals concur that many care homes in England are running at capacity.[1] Most care homes are privately owned by individuals, partnerships or companies. A diminishing number are still run by local authorities, and some by charities, religious organisations and housing associations. Care homes for the elderly are usually either nursing homes that provide 24-hour nursing care by qualified staff, or residential homes supported by GPs or community nurses. A few are dual-registered homes that provide both nursing and residential care.

Care homes are all different from one another

With thousands of care homes being run by different people, there is bound to be a wide range in the quality and diversity of care. All registered care homes have to comply with legislative regulations, and they have similar aims in the kinds of care services they provide. There the similarities end. The claim that every care home is unique is true. Different owners, managers and staff make that a certainty, as no two people are the same, and the caring sector is all about people.

There are other contrasts. Care homes come in all shapes and sizes – from small cottage-type dwellings, converted guest houses, ancient vicarages and stately country mansions to modern, purpose-built units, with some resembling small hotels. Interiors may be homely, rambling, clinical or luxurious. The grounds may provide vistas of sweeping lawns, lily ponds, rose gardens, patios, walkways and convenient benches or a tiny patch squeezed into urban surroundings. All these features influence the particular individuality of each care home.

How care homes are run and managed

Every care home has to have a registered owner (whether an individual, partnership or company) and a registered manager. The manager – or 'person in charge' – is responsible for the overall delivery of care by the home. Often the owner and the manager are one and the same: the owner-manager. Many of the smaller care homes for the elderly are run by owner-managers. Such a person has to combine the administrative work of the home with organising and directing all its care services. The manager of a large corporate organisation is able to delegate responsibilities and obtain support and advice for policies and decisions.

The importance of a good manager cannot be overstated. The particular quality of care provided by the home depends primarily on how well its aims, standards and directions are delivered by the manager. It is the manager who is involved in the day-to-day operations, and who sets the tone and ethos of the home. A manager should provide clear, positive leadership that promotes sound policies and practices by the staff, and delivers inclusive services to residents as well as support to their families.

Care homes must, by law, comply with the government standards set out in the Care Standards 2000 Act and the Health and Social Care (Community Health and Standards) 2003 Act.

The Care Standards Act created the 'National Care Standards Commission', an independent body that has taken over regulation of health and social care services from local councils and health authorities. This Act also allowed the government to set minimum standards and provide detailed regulations covering all aspects of residential care that must be obeyed by law.

The Acts also set out 'National Minimum Standards' that, though not legal requirements, serve as a guide by which the National Care Standards Commission can determine whether each care home meets the needs of its residents. National minimum standards cover the following areas:

- choice of home
- health and personal care
- daily life and social activities
- complaints and protection
- environment
- staffing
- management and administration.

The Commission for Social Care[2] is an independent inspectorate of all social care in England. It was created by the Health and Social Care (Community Health and Standards) 2003 Act mentioned above. It provides guidance on interpretation of the National Minimum Standards and emphasises the need to use them as a target to be exceeded rather than aimed for. In its role as the Commission for Social Care Inspection (CSCI) it carries out inspections of all residential homes in the UK to ensure that the care provided is safe and complies with the legal requirements described.

It should be noted that regulation of this area changes frequently – the Health and Social Care Bill 2007 proposed the amalgamation of the CSCI with the bodies currently responsible for regulating health care in hospitals and mental health facilities to create the Care Quality Commission – an integrated regulator for health and social care.

How managers are appointed

Most current managers have come up 'though the ranks' with little or no management training. Their knowledge and skills have developed though practical experience of care and often a supervisory role in working with adults. Many have had no qualifications apart from those who are first level registered nurses.

Care for the elderly has become more complex. Residents in homes are on average older and many are frailer than in the past. There is a growing need for education on age-related change and a better understanding of the medical features of degenerative conditions and mental impairments. There should be recognition that care for older people involves more than meeting their medical or physical needs, and requires regular opportunities for leisure, cultural and social activities that have been proved to contribute to their improved health and well-being. Training in dealing with these matters is needed at all staff levels, but the first priority is to train the managers who will then be able to improve the skills of the staff they are supervising.

Staffing

Nothing affects residents more than the care they receive from the staff. Those who look after them, tend to their personal needs, talk to them, comfort them, inform them, make them laugh and help them feel emotionally secure, must be all important.

Care homes staff, therefore, need special skills. They should be good communicators, understand the affects of the ageing process and be sensitive to the needs of people who have had to give up much of their former life-styles. They have to blend compassion with the fostering of independence and confidence, and to encourage participation in activities and personal interests.

At the same time, they must be competent in the many aspects of personal care, and in dealing with a wide range of clinical needs of the elderly, ranging from disabilities to dementia. Essential routines may include keeping care plans, making risk assessments, observing health and safety regulations and dealing with accidents and emergencies.

There should be an awareness that residents should be able to maintain their personal identities in respect of their culture, race, ethnic origins and religion. This summary of the basic knowledge and skills that are required by care home staff indicates the standards that should be expected. Are they being met?

Apart from a qualified owner, manager or matron, and the quota of trained staff for nursing homes, the bulk of personal and routine nursing tasks is usually provided by care assistants. Until recently the majority of these staff were unqualified. In the late 1990s a national training organisation for social care was set up to address this problem. Under its current guise, 'Skills for Care', it provides funding and guidance for care sector workforce development and training. As a result the percentage of care home staff who now have some form of relevant qualification has increased dramatically: a survey carried out in 2008 by the Skill Sector Council found that 69 per cent of the 750,000 care workers in the UK are now trained to at least NVQ level 2 with only 10 per cent having no qualifications at all – a reversal of the situation ten years ago.[3]

Despite this, many care homes are finding it increasingly difficult to recruit and retain committed staff. The previous practice of employing unskilled workers at minimal costs implies that care work is 'something anyone can do'. The image of the care worker must continue to be given proper recognition through training and qualifications.

Notes

1. Social Care Provision in England (2008) (available at: www.csci.org.uk/professional, accessed 15 September 2008)
2. www.csci.org.uk (accessed 15 September 2008)
3. Skills for Care 'Media information.' (available at: www.skillsforcare.org.uk/files/Media%20Information(1).pdf, accessed 12 April 2008)

3

How Old is Old?

Times have changed for the old. They are no longer 'as old' as their forebears. This is because of the increase in life expectancy. A century ago it was around 40 years; at the beginning of the 21st century it has become an average of 75 years for men and 80 years for women. Many are now living well past these ages. Improved health care, better living and working conditions, and medical advances that increase survival rates are responsible and are likely to continue. 'Old age' as related to chronological figures has changed. Many people in their 70s and 80s resemble the 60-year-olds of the past.

However, although people are generally living longer, the ageing process is one of degeneration and this can cause a number of physical or psychiatric conditions to develop. These can include arthritis, stroke, heart disease, Parkinson's disease, dementia, depression, and impaired sight or hearing. Added to which can be non-specific problems usually termed 'general frailty'. It is a long list and any of the conditions listed may lead to dependency and the need for a person to receive daily care as a resident in a care home.

There is a misconception that older people belong to a special tribe, all with the same problems, opinions and attitudes. Yet older people are just as different from each other as are members of younger generational groups. How can it be otherwise in view of the wide range of different experiences everyone has as their life progresses from childhood to old age? There are differences formed by family backgrounds, education, careers and relationships. All these help shape a person's character and outlook on life. This does not confer superior virtues on the elderly. They may have wisdom, good humour and tolerance, but are just as likely to be cantankerous, boring and narrow minded. Like everyone else, the old are a mixed bunch, but each is an individual with their own particular interests and personality.

In their years before retirement, many people choose to take part in a wide variety of leisure pursuits. Some familiar ones include gardening, sports, keep fit, DIY, drama, photography, dressmaking, pottery, art, computing, dancing, singing, local history, creative writing, yoga, fishing, antiques, astronomy, foreign languages.

People choose to take part in such interests because they provide enjoyable and interesting creative alternatives to their work, and often contribute a real quality to their lives. It is, however, a sad fact that many people give them up after retirement despite having abundant leisure time. There are various reasons, including having less income, a fear of going out and difficulties with transport. However, the most over-riding reason is the insidious loss of a daily routine, which removes the impetus to continue a more active life.

Old people at home and who remain mobile will still engage in the occupations of everyday living. They will have their home to care for, perhaps a garden to tend, they will go shopping, visit the post office, the library, perhaps take the dog for its walks, and visit or be visited by family and friends. These common routines not only are essential for survival, they provide purpose and meaning for people's lives. They involve exercise, planning, choice and communication, all of which can result in the maintaining of self-esteem and satis-faction with their role. They represent some of the 'activities' that people often say they miss when they go into a care home.

When more structured activities are considered there is a need to understand how the ageing process has affected each person. Recent life events such as loss of a partner or health deterioration may make them dismiss choices on offer.

4

Why Activities are Needed

The term 'activities' can include a vast range of everyday occasions, communications, tasks or occupations of the sort that we all take part in. Activities are not solely concerned with personal interests or organised pursuits such as arts and crafts, however useful they are.

Taking part in activities is doing something rather than doing nothing. An activity can be as commonplace as a friendly chat, a family reminiscence, doing a crossword together, playing cards, or looking through a newspaper. These occasions are not to be dismissed or undervalued: they are valuable links with real life.

Is it considered that a person in residential care must be so old, so frail, so dependent that they do virtually nothing each day? In many care homes it is assumed that the needs of personal and clinical care, the meal times, the visits by a chiropodist, a hairdresser and perhaps the vicar, and weekly sessions of bingo and community singing are sufficient for 'an activities programme'. In between these events what do they do all day? Nothing.

For people of any age there is a need to be occupied in purposeful activity. The daily tasks and routines we undertake each day may not appear to be making a contribution to the quality of our life, and we often regard some of them as irksome. But they are an integral part of the driving force of our existence. Humans were designed to be mentally and physically active creatures. The things we have to do or we choose to do will usually be a mix of routines, duties, interests and leisure pursuits. Whether they are pleasurable, satisfying or boring, they are significant components in the structure of our lives. When we wake in the mornings we know what we are likely to be doing that day. There will probably be plans for other days ahead. The conception of our existence is built around future activities. Imagine if we were suddenly deprived of most or all of these daily occupations and the expectations of future happenings.

This is the situation that most residents in care homes have to face. For some with severe disabilities or frailty it may be a relief after struggling to cope at home to receive personal care and no longer have the worry of cooking and housework. But the danger is that providing excessive care leads to total dependence, which may not be entirely necessary. Encouraging the retention of any ability to perform personal care, exercising choices in selecting clothes and food, and finding ways of overcoming physical problems, help to maintain independence.

There needs to be a more integrated approach to care. Activity methods can be incorporated in the basic personal and clinical care regime. The provision of activities of any kind should not be regarded as an 'extra', 'a treat' or 'a change': they should be made a vital component of the whole caring process.

In a minority of homes such methods can be witnessed, often led by enthusiastic managers who involve their staff in providing a variety of occupations for the residents. The results are seen in the lively conversations, the cheerful interaction between residents and staff and the improved morale of the latter. Often volunteers from residents' families have been recruited and they too clearly enjoy helping.

These methods are not the result of new and revolutionary ideas. The advantages of providing activities for elderly patients in hospital was highlighted as long ago as 1958[1] when studies suggested that 'activity nursing' could help meet a patient's psychological and social needs through mental stimulation in activity programmes.

Lack of stimulation and activity can result in detrimental physical and psychological changes. Physical changes include:

- loss of muscle tone
- increased risk of osteoporosis
- increased risk of respiratory tract infections
- constipation
- increased risk of deep vein thrombosis
- poor appetite and difficulty in sleeping.

Psychological changes include:

- poor concentration
- increased confusion
- disrupted sleep patterns
- increased risk of depression.

Providing activities for care home residents not only reduces the physical risks associated with immobility and lack of stimulation, but has also been shown to produce improvements in behaviour, cognition and sleep patterns. During the decades that followed Pappas, Curtis and Baker's original study (see note 1), work has been carried out in the UK and

USA on such methods, and it has become recognised that activity programmes can result in important therapeutic effects in patient care.[2,3] Designing regular daily activities suited to the needs and abilities of patients has been shown to result in improvement in emotional responsiveness, perception, alertness and overall enjoyment. It has been found that activity programmes can alleviate the boredom,[4] apathy and depression that so often exist in elderly patients, and can help to improve sleep patterns.[5]

Attitudes towards the care of the elderly in residential settings have changed gradually over the last 20 years. The increasing numbers of very elderly and frail residents in care homes has compelled care to become more concerned with the quality of life being offered than in the earlier more impersonal approaches. Even so, while there has been a much wider awareness of the occupational needs of elderly residents in care, there has not been an overall take-up of activity methods throughout the sector.

There are still too many instances of neglect and inadequate care of the most vulnerable who, because of severe frailty, confusion or dementia, are often isolated and do not receive the frequent attention they should be given. Relatives and friends who visit are often distressed to find their loved ones showing signs of incontinence, with remains of uneaten food. The cause is usually insufficient or inadequately trained staff and lack of supervision by the management. Examples of such poor practice are reminiscent of the worst aspects of the institutional regimes of the past and are totally unacceptable in care homes today. Such homes need to be revitalised.

The case for regulating activity provision

There is currently no legislation in the UK that specifically requires care homes for the elderly to provide activities. The Care Standard Act of 2000, which defined the National Minimum Standards, gave a brief, general recommendation in Standard 12 that residents should 'be given opportunities for stimulation through leisure and recreational activities'. There are no examples or suggestions of what this means, no guidance of best practice, no directions of staff involvement or suggestions concerning the employment of a responsible organiser of activities. It is therefore left to managers to choose whether to provide a comprehensive programme of activities or to take up the all too familiar option of arranging a few group entertainments. Many of the residents will be intelligent, talented and discerning. They do not deserve to be grouped as infants.

The government has recently gone some way to giving this area the recognition it deserves. In 2006 the Department of Health asked the National Institute for Clinical Excellence (NICE) to produce guidance for primary and residential care on interventions that promote the mental well-being of older people. Draft guidance was issued in 2007[6] – this is currently in the subject of consultation and formal guidance is expected to be issued in October 2008. The draft guidance focuses on the role of occupational therapy and physical activity in the promotion of mental well-being in later life. The draft guidance includes recommendations that adults living in residential care should be offered:

- exercise programmes led by trained exercise instructors at least 1–2 times per week

- the opportunity to participate in community walking schemes.

The guidance also recommends that those working with older people should receive training in occupational therapy and communication skills.

While there is yet no widespread acceptance of the need to make activities an integral part of care, there has developed in many homes a general awareness that 'something should be done'. Current inspection reports usually include comments on the extent of activities being provided. Care homes are expected to display their 'activity programme'. But, although inspection reports will include a statement on the extent of the activities, there is little judgement given as to their content or how successful they are. A much more precise and compulsory requirement for a regular programme should be established for each home to measure what is being provided to comply with Standard 12.

What activities?

The lack of specified suggestions for activities in the minimum standards can be attributed to the fact that it is not possible or desirable to recommend a programme that would be suitable for every care home. The vast differences in the capabilities of the residents, the available facilities, the interests of an organiser and the staff, and the environment of the home all affect the choice of activities to use. Each home needs to produce its own personalised programme of activities, but the greatest need is for a completely new approach to the whole subject.

How to introduce person-centred care

The decision to introduce person-centred care needs careful planning and the realisation that it will not be an easy or swift process, especially if the home is run on traditional lines. Some essentials to be considered are listed below:

- Total commitment to the process is needed at all levels of management.

- Care staff need to be engaged and their role in achieving change outlined in detail.

- A monitoring system needs to be in place to revise the plan should problems arise.

- A training programme needs to be in place for all staff.

- Do not fear failure.

Notes

1. Pappas, W., Curtis, W.P. and Baker, J. (1958) 'A controlled study of an intensive treatment programme for hospitalized geriatric patients.' *Journal of the American Geriatrics Society 6*, 17–25.

2. Gibson, F. (1989) *Using Reminiscence.* London: Help the Aged, pp.9–10.

3. Baines, S., Saxby, P. and Ehlert, K. (1987) 'Reality orientation and reminiscence therapy.' *British Journal of Psychiatry 151*, 222–231.

4. Turner, P. (1993) 'Activity nursing and the changes in the quality of life of elderly patients: A semi-quantitative study.' *Journal of Advanced Nursing 18*, 1727–1733.

5. Richards, K.C., Beck, C., O'Sullivan, P.S. and Shue, V.H. (2005) 'Effect of individualized social activity on sleep in nursing home residents with dementia.' *Journal of the American Geriatrics Society 53*, 1510–1517.

6. NICE (2008) *Public Health Draft Guidance* (available at: www.nice.org.uk/nicemedia/pdf/MentalWellbeingOlder%20 PeopleDraftGuidanceConsultation.pdf, accessed 12 April 2008.)

Further reading

Allen, C. and Bennett, A. (1984) 'Long-stay geriatric care.' *Nursing Mirror 158*, 15, 1–4.

Cosin, L.Z., Mort, M., Post, F., Westropp, C. and Williams, M. (1958) 'Experimental treatment for persistent senile confusion.' *International Journal of Social Psychiatry 4*, 24–42.

Feil, N. (1989) *Validation Therapy.* Bicester, Oxfordshire: Winslow Press.

Folsom, J.C. (1968) 'Reality orientation for the elderly mental patient.' *Journal of Geriatric Psychiatry 1*, 291–307.

Gessert, V.G. and Klay, G. (1984) 'The evolving role of the activity co-coordinator.' *American Health Care Association Journal 10*, 3, 67–70.

5

The Activities Organiser

In the past little priority has been given to providing comprehensive activities in care homes. The need to provide physical care for dependent residents has predominated, giving little or no provision for any forms of occupations or activities. The practice, of some homes, of giving responsibility for arranging activities to an existing staff member – often a care assistant who has shown interest in the work – is seldom successful. It is difficult to prepare and carry out anything other than hasty and often ad hoc activities as additional to everyday care duties. During absences or other pressures, activities often have to be sacrificed. If activities are to be taken seriously and made part of the home's care, there is a need to employ an organiser with responsibility for planning and carrying out the detailed work of a comprehensive programme.

With the increasing recognition by health and social service authorities, as well as the National Care Standards Commission, for the need for occupational and leisure activities in care homes, the employment of activities organisers is steadily increasing.

The introduction of the policy should come from the registered manager and the owner of the home, unless they are one and the same person. The attitude of a committed management towards promoting a stimulating activities programme is crucial to a successful care home. As well as the appointment of a suitable organiser, there will be the need for the provision of the resources required, and engagement of the staff in supporting these aims.

Qualities and skills

Being an organiser is a complex job. No two homes are the same, and the extent of the work will depend on the category of the care provided, the expectations of the management and the home's environment. It is likely that in many homes the appointment of an organiser will be their first, with no previous experience of the impact of the role on the staff. Lack of experience need not deter an applicant who finds the prospect of the work interesting and challenging. There may have to be an element of learning on the job. However, in the initial stage, personal qualities needed include:

- being a good communicator
- having imagination and creative ideas
- understanding the needs of older people
- being self-confident and resourceful
- having the ability to be a team leader
- having tolerance and a sense of humour.

Experience should include:

- interest in creative activities such as art, craft, music or writing
- experience in dealing with the effects of physical or mental disabilities

- interest in occupational, leisure and outdoor activities and outings

- interest in engaging with local services, libraries, museums and community groups.

A newly appointed organiser will need a period of essential preparation. Discussions with the manager and senior staff will enable a policy to be established and agreed.

Induction and training

Training for the work of an organiser may be provided by the home, but it is more likely that it will have to be found in external courses. The development of such courses is under way and details of what is available are given at the end of this chapter. Books and publications that discuss the value of activities for the elderly should be studied, and visits should be made to other homes or venues where these practices can be seen.

Information on the techniques involved in the activities that are suggested in this book is readily available in libraries, and the topics covered are often offered in local community education courses.

Profiles and history of residents

In the early stages it will be valuable to make individual profiles of each resident. These should cover the present abilities and potential of the person. While any impairments of a physical or mental nature should be noted, they should be viewed in as positive a light as possible.

The past history of a resident is even more important. The interests, work and experiences of a person provide a reference to their individuality and a pointer to the activities that they may choose to follow. Talking to the residents and to the staff who have regular contact with them, as well as reading their care plans, will supply a range of useful information. The views of relatives or friends of a resident can also be invited after explaining the purpose of the enquiry.

The records of residents from ethnic minority groups need particular care so that their opportunities to partake in social and leisure activities are the same as everybody else's. They may have special interests or skills that can contribute much to the variety of a care home.

It should always be remembered that the information in care plans and written profiles of residents is confidential and should only be available to the staff or authorised officials.

Responsibility for resources

An organiser will be responsible for the different items that will be needed for running activities. These could include:

- Equipment – audio, visual, music, sports, games, leisure.

- Materials – arts and crafts, writing, displays.

- Gardening – seeds, plants, containers, tools.

- Reminiscence – pictures, books, props, materials.

- Cookery – ingredients, recipes, utensils.

There will be a need to collect, maintain, record and store these resources. An activities budget and accounts will be required. It may be possible to obtain many items through bargain shops, market stalls and car boot sales. Some items may be obtained from the residents or their relatives, or by advertising in the local press. Otherwise, fundraising events to pay for needed items are always an option.

Other responsibilities that are likely to come the way of an organiser are the library, the supply of newspapers and magazines, arranging social events and seasonal occasions and outings.

An organiser could not be expected to be immediately responsible for a full programme of activities and all the other duties as described in this outline. These represent possibilities that depend on a number of conditions including the number and category of the residents and whether the post is a full- or part-time contract.

The development of an activities programme has to be a progressive process and one that should include the whole staff, the residents themselves and their relatives. Hold a meeting for residents and their relatives and tell them of the plans that are proposed and invite any of the latter who may be interested to help or contribute any skills they have to the programme.

Contact local libraries, schools, churches, community centres, Age Concern and other care homes and discuss the possibility of arranging events with two-way interactions. Use the internet to gain information or support from local and national services.

Training

NAPA – the National Association for Providers of Activities for Older People – offer bespoke training courses for all levels of care home staff, including distance learning courses and City & Guilds. Members receive a newsletter three times a year which gives information, ideas, reviews or details of books on activities and courses throughout the country. Publications include *The New Culture of Therapeutic Activity with Older People*[1] and information leaflet packs. Tel: 020 7078 9375; www.napa-activities.co.uk

Note

1. Perrin, T., NAPA (2004) *The New Culture of Therapeutic Activity with Older People.* (Avaliable at from NAPA Bondway Commercial Centre, Unit 5.12, 5th fl, 11 Bondway, London SW8 1SQ tel 0207 078 9378 www.napa-activities.co.uk/publications) Speechmark Publishing Ltd.)

6

Arranging the Programme

An activities programme cannot be pre-designed. It has to be formed around the particular needs of the residents, the general culture of the home, and its resources and environment. Making a haphazard list must be avoided. There needs to be careful planning. A structure is required that gives guidelines for producing a programme that will be appropriate to the abilities of the residents and show purpose in its aims.

What do we want activities to achieve for residents?

- interest
- enjoyment
- fulfilment
- self-confidence
- satisfaction
- independence
- choice.

Is this too much to hope for? Let's not be too ambitious – but accept that if an activity provides any one of these qualities it is worth doing. Each activity can be considered in its main category of application such as:

- occupational
- creative
- physical
- leisure/recreation.

Some activities will overlap these categories, but that is no disadvantage for this is mainly an exercise in defining a general plan.

Decide what the likely benefits will be

- *Cognitive development:* Stimulate memory, awaken reminiscence, encourage reasoning, imagination and decision making.

- *Creative skills:* Revive previous interests, encourage new ventures, stimulate a spirit of achievement.

- *Physical abilities:* Maintain or improve mobility and dexterity and give a sense of well-being.

- *Enjoyment:* Meet cultural interests, experience a sense of fun, be competitive, share interaction with other residents, provide relaxation from stress or boredom.

Selecting activities

When you select any activity consider these aspects:

- Will it be suitable for group or individual work or both?

- How many residents are likely to be interested?

- Will it be suitable or need to be adapted for those who have impairments?

- Will there be a need for material resources and a suitable venue?

- Will you need any help from staff or volunteers?

- When can it be held during the day and how often?

Balancing the programme

The final arrangement should provide a variety of different activities that offer choice and liveliness. A balanced programme should include:

- individual and group activities

- regular group activities on a weekly basis

- short informal sessions

- physical activities, exercise and games

- occupational tasks

- cultural interests

- outings – local and further afield.

Such a range will include sessions for groups for an hour upwards and involve the use of materials and equipment with a mix of short, informal get-togethers for discussions, poems and puzzles that will supply a fund of topics for conversations and exchange of views.

Cultural interests that involve religion, visits to concerts, plays and films, exhibitions and gardens should be made available as the opportunities occur.

The choices

The choice is vast. In the first instance select those that you have the most confidence in running and in which residents have expressed an interest. The activities outlined in this book have been shown to be successful and give residents interest and enjoyment. Do not take on more than can be managed at the outset. It will then be easier to increase or change the topics as you wish.

Keeping a record

The home may require a record to be kept of the daily activities and may need health and safety regulations to be filled. It is especially useful in the early stages to keep a record of each session and evaluate its success or failings. Be realistic about your aims and the results. Record such basic points as:

- Was it understood?
- Did it provide interest?
- Did it stimulate ideas, talk, comment?
- Were physical/mental abilities engaged?
- Were sitting arrangements, equipment and materials satisfactory?
- Did members get on with one another?
- Did they want to come back for more?
- Did you enjoy it?
- Will the next session need any changes?

Detailed records can be reduced as experience develops and as regular practice creates similar results. There is a case for making a general review from time to time of the main activities, to consider what has been achieved and to make plans for the future.

It is too much to hope that an activities programme will be a success from the start. It will emerge from the committed efforts of the organiser and the staff by shaping activities to the interests and abilities of the residents. This is a learning process for everybody – how to enable the elderly and the frail to tackle, explore and enjoy being active in a care home.

7

$\mathcal{A}$ctivities

One to one

Activities should be for everybody, but some people don't like being in a group. There may be a number of different reasons for this:

- An elderly person who has lived on their own for a long period may have become withdrawn and lost the wish to socialise.

- The trauma of moving into care, leaving familiar surroundings and becoming part of a new and strange community can cause some residents to remain apart.

- Some people may have always been reluctant to mix with others or join social groups.

- Some may be hampered by impairments of speech, hearing or sight, any of which may make communication difficult, especially in a group.

Whatever the reason, everyone has the right of freedom of choice and should never be expected to take up an activity if they do not wish to, especially if their condition makes it difficult or embarrassing for them.

It is possible that, after seeing what is offered, some people may eventually change their mind and take part. In the meantime, it is important not to neglect anyone who does not take part in group activities, and they should never be left in lonely isolation. They need to be given individual activities.

With average staff levels, it may well be difficult to find time for available staff to have regular individual sessions with particular residents. However, there is usually a friendly rapport between care assistants and the residents they look after on a regular basis. These occasions should be used whenever possible to encourage residents to talk and exchange views and opinions on a variety of topics. The quiet, unassuming person can be deceptive. They may have had a whole range of experiences, but even in an uneventful life there are interesting comparisons to be made with past times and the present. The young and the old have much to learn from each other.

There need be no shortage of subjects:

- Memories, past and present:
  - Childhood, family life, schooldays, friends, adventures, food, clothes, travel, work, relationships and marriage, children, sport, hobbies, entertainment, celebrities, TV, newspapers, politics and so on.

- Thoughts about:
  - Dreams, star predictions, superstitions, the best age, names for children, the best pets, advertisements, war, drugs, traffic and so on.

Have a supply of:

- Newspapers – national and local – and magazines that provide topics to talk about and discuss.

- Large-print crosswords to start together.

- Cassette tapes or CDs to play and listen to together.

- Talking books – discuss the story.

- Poetry anthologies – ones with a poem for every day of the year could provide useful topics.

Other easily arranged activities include:

- memory games

- word games, hangman

- alphabet games – flowers, towns.

8

*T*alking and Listening

Communication is something most of us do every day without giving it any thought. For elderly residents in a care home effective communication is an activity that is vital to their daily lives. Its simplest and best form is carried out through a one-to-one relationship, and is all about talking and listening to one another. Communication is the basis for developing essential bonds between staff and residents. It sounds easy but some people are better at it than others.

Some residents may have little to say for a variety of reasons. If they have lived on their own for a long period, they may have lost the facility to talk easily. Others may have hearing difficulties, suffer from the effects of a stroke, or have various forms of confusion, any of which may make listening or speaking difficult. These special problems need guidance and advice by a speech and language therapist. Such residents should never be ignored or left in silence because of their problems.

All residents, whether they have special communication needs or not, should be given opportunities to express their thoughts, make their wishes and choices known, and state their needs and opinions. Care assistants who usually do the bulk of personal care have a special responsibility in developing a resident's confidence and trust. It is to their credit that so many are able to establish a warm and friendly bond between themselves and residents despite the wide age differences that exist. There is a constant need to respect dignity, to provide privacy and avoid being patronising or over-familiar, yet to remain on good terms.

This demands good communication skills that may come naturally or have to be learned through training in the home. We convey our feelings through the tone of our voice, making eye contact with a listener, through our facial expressions, our gestures, the way we stand and walk. Being a considerate listener is just as important. Some elderly people are slow and hesitant in speech because they cannot remember some words. They need time, encouragement and understanding responses from a patient listener. As their confidence grows their speech is likely to improve.

The keyworker scheme that exists in many care homes in which assistants attend the same group of residents is especially useful in developing good talking and listening practices. This regular individual attention is a valuable support for a resident. It provides a close link for a resident with somebody they come to rely on and who may well fill the role of a substitute family member.

Care plans

A care plan is a continuous record of a resident's health and social needs and progress. It should not only give an assessment of medical conditions and the level of care needed, but also provide information on the person's life history. It is useful to produce a profile of an individual's personality, career and past interests or skills.

Much of this information can be gathered by the regular conversations a resident has with the person they see most: the care assistant. Through these informal exchanges information can be built up on the resident's background, education, family, work, interests and skills. It is often revealing to hear of the wide variety of experiences a person has had: the good, the bad, the humdrum, the joys, and often the pain and the suffering. The essentials that affect a resident's social needs – their past interests, work and hobbies – should be recorded. This information will be valuable not only in choosing topics to talk about but also in selecting suitable activities. It should be emphasised that a care plan and the information it contains is private and confidential.

Special problems

Some residents who have severe difficulties in speech and language need special individual attention. This includes anyone with impaired hearing or poor sight, and those who have suffered a stroke, or developed Parkinson's disease or dementia. Activities for such people need to be remedial as much as social. Advice from a speech therapist should be obtained for guiding or helping residents with such problems. Too often their inability to take part in regular communication leads to isolation and depression. Methods are needed that help to restore confidence and to establish friendly relationships.

Some general guidelines to use

Hearing difficulties

- Turn off background sounds from radio or TV.
- Face the person so that they can lip-read words if they are able.
- Speak fairly slowly and clearly without shouting.

- Use short sentences.

- Use gestures, smiles, frowns and eye movements to emphasise words and meanings.

- If there is no understanding, repeat the words in a different way or write them down.

- Praise and encourage their responses.

Visual impairment

- Face the person at eye level.

- Use gentle touch – on hands or arm – to establish contact.

- Say the person's name and say who you are.

- Speak calmly and clearly to give reassurance.

- When confidence is established, choose simple basic subjects to begin a conversation – the day, the season, the weather.

- Encourage responses; overcome inhibitions with good humour.

- Give things to touch and hold. To distinguish different shapes use, for example, an orange and a lemon, a potato and a tomato, a ballpoint and a pencil. Also give them leaves, bark, shells and so on to feel and to talk about.

- When there is some vision use large-print books, clear pictures without too much detail, and audio tapes.

Other speech and language problems

These include dysphasia – usually caused by a stroke – which affects the ability either to understand what is said or to use meaningful speech. Another problem that affects speech is dysarthria, caused by a number of diseases that affect the brain or central nervous system. The person knows what to say but has difficulty in producing the words.

These acute conditions require advice and guidance from a speech therapist on the best methods of improving communication with the person.

In considering the provision of pleasurable activities for people with severe impairments or disabilities, there needs to be an understanding of their basic needs. How can their personal world be expanded to help them regain a sense of well-being and the sharing of everyday experiences and interests? It is not easy, but not impossible.

It needs commitment to make their lives less institutionalised, less confined, less disengaged from the basic elements of life. It can be expected that they will receive high quality medical and personal care, but, because of their dependent condition and the limitations of a care home, they will often lack the stimulation they need.

Too often these people may remain marooned in their bedroom, being visited infrequently – mainly for meals and personal care. They need to be taken out of their room regularly: to visit other residents, to see the view from the other windows, to go out into the garden, or down the road to the park or the shops, to see the sky, the trees, smell the grass and the flowers, hear the sounds of birds, dogs, traffic, children, feel the wind, touch leaves and bark and acorns and conkers. All residents need these experiences, but it is a particular requirement for the most dependent members of a care home.

Some homes do manage to take residents out on simple outings, but for many it is attempted only infrequently or not at all. Lack of sufficient staff to make it possible is the usual reason. To overcome this there should be a general request for help from relatives or other volunteers who could accompany a staff member on making visits outside the home.

9

*K*eep Moving

Take a look at an 'average' care home and consider what is going on inside:

- Are the residents doing anything during the day?

- Are they spending a large part of the day mainly sitting, sleeping, and having snacks and meals?

- How independent are they? How many of them can walk on their own or with a walking stick?

- Are they encouraged, if they are able, to look after themselves: to dress and undress, wash, go to the toilet, feed themselves, care for their room?

- Do any of them who are able help in the running of the home: preparing and clearing up in the dining room, distributing post or newspapers, keeping the library, arranging flower displays?

The need for residents to be kept mobile and active is vital for their own benefit and future, and helps reduce the workload of the care staff. Before coming into care, older people have to be active to carry out tasks for their everyday needs. If they have not developed a disabling disease such as a severe form of arthritis, suffered a stroke or Parkinsons disease, any lack of mobility is more likely to be the result of being inactive.

The person who spends long periods sitting and unoccupied, develops weak muscles and bones, and inefficient heart and lungs. Physical deterioration can often lead to decreased mental ability and depression.

Unfortunately, the regime in many care homes does little to maintain or improve mobility. Their 'care' removes the need for residents to perform the everyday tasks they did in their own homes. They no longer have to prepare meals, do the washing or housework, go shopping or do gardening. These simple activities help to keep an older person both physically and mentally alert. In a care home these tasks are done for them. The armchairs await, and long periods of daily inactivity can result in the beginnings of immobility. Once this has set in it is often difficult and sometimes impossible to restore free movement. The old saying 'use it, or lose it' still holds good.

Developing independence

Soon after residents are admitted to a care home it is crucial to encourage them to remain as active as possible. Careful assessment of a person's capabilities with information from either the GP or primary care team and relatives will help to show what activities in daily life and personal care they are likely to be able to do. Care assistants can then aid and supervise a resident to maintain this level and perhaps improve it.

Some residents with greater physical or mental disabilities will require more help than others, but offering to do everything for them may make them far more dependent than is necessary or good for them.

A general, but flexible form of support should try to encourage a resident to do as many as possible of the following tasks:

- dress and undress

- get in and out of bed

- wash and use the toilet

- use a shower

- if there are facilities, make a hot drink

- feed themselves

- keep their room tidy.

Doing any of these tasks may for some be difficult and slow. What is important is the achievement, which gives dignity and independence and the maintenance of mobility. Better for them to try and succeed by muddling through, than to give up. Regular reassessment will be necessary to check that levels of mobility are maintained.

Walking

The ability to walk alone is a priceless asset. It provides independence of movement and allows a resident to make choices – when to go to the toilet, the dining room, the sitting room or garden. It gives freedom and confidence and contributes to an improved mental attitude. It also frees care assistants to be able to give more attention to the dependent residents who most need their help. Even some of these may not need to be condemned to a wheelchair; a walking aid may be the answer. Often slight unsteadiness can be overcome with a walking stick – either a metal adjustable crutch or an ordinary wooden walking stick. The correct length is important and it should be adjusted so that, while the person is standing, the handle is level with the top of the thigh, the elbow is slightly bent and the shoulders are level. A wooden stick may need to be shortened by sawing off a piece from the end and fixing a rubber ferrule on it to prevent the stick from slipping.

Often the fear of falling has to be overcome at first, but, with daily supervised practice and encouragement, success-ful walking can bring confidence. For those who are more dependent, a walking frame may be needed. Various types can be obtained – some with wheels – and most have bags attached to carry necessities. Providing it is of the correct height for the person, a frame gives firm support and is another means of providing independence for a person to walk alone. Using a walking aid may be slow and a struggle for the person, but if it promotes mobility it is worth it. In dif-ficult cases advice on the most suitable aid should be obtained from an occupational therapist or physiotherapist.

Residents should be encouraged to walk regularly, either on their own or with minimal supervision. It should be part of every mobile person's daily routine to go for a 20 minute walk around the home or, when suitable, in the gardens. There will be a need for organisation at meal times, which should not become the familiar wheelchair races to save time. Allowing residents their independence in walking alone as often as possible is invaluable to their self-esteem and reduces the demands of transporting them for their every need.

Find ways of getting residents to move at other times, such as:

- Stop bringing tea or coffee directly to them if they are capable of walking. Put such refreshments in another place to which they will have to walk.

- Wherever possible arrange activities in another area or room away from the main sitting area.

- Use the garden whenever the weather is suitable – for refreshments, a picnic, smelling the flowers, spotting the birds, looking at the sky, or walking with friends, relatives or staff.

Activities

Keep fit exercises

These sessions should be run by a leader who has received training, can provide suitable exercises for older people and is aware of the precautions to be taken for those with some medical conditions. Sessions can range from 'sitting down' exercises to those that involve more extensive movements for residents with greater mobility. Local courses are often available for anyone interested in receiving training. Alternatively, arrangements may be made for regular visits by a qualified therapist.

Informal activities

Care staff, relatives or qualified volunteers can easily run simple activities and games that require minimal preparation. These can provide sessions that involve movement and physical judgement and help to maintain mobility. The recreational aspect of games is often preferred by some who dislike structured, 'keep fit' exercises.

The following suggestions are suitable for residents with reasonable mobility, but also for some with physical impairments who wish to join in, including determined wheelchair occupants. Precautions must obviously be taken for anyone whose medical condition might be aggravated by an activity, and where necessary to obtain a doctor's opinion as to whether they should take part.

- Throwing, catching different sized balls or balloons – to a leader, to each other or over a dividing line between two groups.

- Indoor or outdoor bowls or skittles.

- Throwing quoits over numbered posts on a board or floor or lawn.

- Outdoor clock golf – the very popular simple outdoor game on grass using plastic puts and cups.

- Crazy golf – a course using home-made obstacles.

- Swing tennis – for one or two players. This involves batting a tennis ball attached by a long tether to an upright post.

- Badminton – batting a shuttlecock across a net or a line.

- Pall mall – a simpler form of croquet. Two hoops are placed in an area of smooth grass. Each player takes turns to drive the ball with a mallet or bat through each hoop in the fewest number of strokes.

- Boules – metal balls are thrown to land as near as possible to a target ball. Plastic balls can be substituted.

- Swimming – one of the best exercises of all as it provides movements that improve suppleness, strength and stamina while supporting the body and avoiding weight-bearing on joints. It can give a person with physical impairments a boost to self-confidence in achieving equal performance with the able-bodied. Local swimming pools often provide periods reserved for elderly or disabled swimmers and it is worth taking small groups with a trained supervisor whenever possible.

10

Role Play

In *As You Like It*, Shakespeare said:

> All the world's a stage,
> And all the men and women merely players...

Can we find ways to encourage elderly people to play a part and to discover the fun and excitement of acting? The answer is that in some centres of care they are already doing it – and there should be much more of it. This is not to propose a drama course requiring acting skills and the learning of lines. There is a simple entry into the world of make-believe that is easily attained and likely to be successful. It is known as role play.

In role play a person can explore through self-expression and the re-living of past experiences, identify with another person, rediscover a younger self and develop imaginative ideas.

It is important at the outset to understand the difference between improvised role play and acting for an audience. Role play is an entirely personal process that aims to develop a person's own ideas in their own way. In role play theatrical limitations do not exist: there is no script, and no directions to follow on movements or speech. Acting for a stage play is controlled by the ideas of the dramatist and is intended to entertain an audience. Role players use their own ideas and are only concerned with themselves – and the other role players.

The principle of role play arises from the primitive need first known in childhood to invent situations and events in which one identifies with another person. Most of us may remember our role as king or queen, hero, tyrant or magician that we took up with enthusiasm when young. This characteristic can still be stimulated and developed through interesting and imaginative role play. The device has been used successfully for many years in education, social, industrial and business training and is eminently suitable for using as an activity with the elderly to explore and enjoy.

Role play can:

- revive personal memories

- help relive experiences that were enjoyable, funny, difficult or puzzling

- help in understanding other people's attitudes

- develop self-confidence

- encourage imaginative ideas

- improve communication skills.

Role play as an activity

In forming a group there will need to be an explanatory talk on what role play is, and how people will take part. Individual approaches will probably be needed to overcome the distrust of the unknown. This will probably be the most difficult part. Promise that it is going to be fun!

The person leading the group should be the one who can evoke responses which will realise the aims of the group.

Ideally such a person should have experience of the performing arts – in drama, dance or music. Someone with such experience might be a member of the staff or an interested relative, but may have to be enrolled from the local community. In time, it may be possible for others without experience to learn the necessary techniques.

Starting points

Make sure you have a large enough room or area that will allow free movement without hindrance or overcrowding. Be prepared for wheelchair players.

After forming a group, choose an event that is likely to evoke clear memories of a familiar experience in which everyone is invited to take part together. It is likely that some may choose to remain as onlookers initially.

The first step in engaging people to take part in improvisation is the most difficult. They may be shy, afraid of making themselves look foolish, or consider the activity childish. But inviting everyone to be part of a scene together gives them protection from feeling self-conscious. A leader should be aware that these feelings are likely to exist at first, and to take an active part in the action and to direct it to create general movement and united efforts.

An example of an approach

A crowd scene

Let's start by acting together a scene that you will have often been part of: a busy shopping street in a town. Find partners, or be on your own. Decide who you are, and what you are doing. Are you:

- Buying or selling items from a street stall?

- In a shop trying on clothes or shoes?

- Playing music to the passers-by?

- Serving in a café?

- Looking for a lost child?

- A driver having an argument with a traffic warden?

The progress of the scene will be helped by the leader giving a running commentary that stimulates interaction by the players by asking questions, such as:

- Is it: raining, cold? Very hot? Windy?

- Are you: carrying heavy bags? Struggling with children?

- Are you: tired? In a hurry? Feeling stressed?

Suggest some happenings

- There has been an accident.

- Someone has been mugged.

- A skateboarder is causing chaos.

- A group is demonstrating: anti-hunting? Anti-war?

Keep the scene short. Stop the action before it runs out of steam. Praise the players' efforts – even if they have been haphazard and disorganised. Remember they have taken an important first step in self-expression, and it will be easier next time.

Continuing the theme

Other crowd scenes should follow, but with an increasing focus on developing more constructive ideas. Discuss beforehand how each group should work together using speech and comment in exchanges to accompany and support the action. Choose subjects that will provide variety and scope for interesting ideas and imaginative action such as:

- a summer fête with sideshows and entertainers
- a fairground
- a crowded beach
- an auction
- a wedding.

In any of these preliminary scenes there will be the need for the leader to give suggestions, helpful directions and constant encouragement. None of the prompts should be prescriptive – make them informal, amusing and with the potential of surprise. As confidence is developed, the leader can afford to be less intrusive, and able to encourage the players to use their own ideas.

Role play in small groups

Having overcome the first tentative steps and provided the experience of playing in crowd scenes, focus the players' actions on particular situations in small groups. Simple scenes can be suggested that require exchanges with another person or persons. Ask if they can think of ways to make the scene more than a mere questions and answers exchange. Can it be made interesting, pose a problem or be made funny?

Working in groups of two or three, improvise a scene on lines such as:

- asking the way in a town or village
- seeing the doctor

- inquiring about a missing pet
- a conversation in a vet's waiting room
- having a picnic with difficulties
- being taught to drive.

If they agree, invite each group to repeat their scene for the other members to watch. Hold a short discussion with constructive comments on how effective the scene was and whether other members have had similar experiences.

Further group work

The next step will probably have to be in the next session. Ask them to think and plan a scene of their own to improvise in their group. Suggest that they choose an event that has happened to them or is familiar to them. If there is a need for ideas, give them some basic characters to use. Do not embellish or provide action or development. Let them do this for themselves. Some suggestions include:

- noisy neighbours
- a door-to-door salesman
- a graffiti sprayer
- a traffic warden
- a fortune teller
- carol singers
- street footballers.

The way ahead

At this stage, role play should have become a well-established activity. Once members have overcome any early inhibitions, they enjoy their newfound interest and will be eager to continue. The emphasis on real-life situations should be maintained. The long lives of elderly people are a rich and varied source for improvised role play scenes. These can give expression to a wide range of feelings, opinions and humour. There is, however, a need to be aware that some topics or situations may invoke sensitive or painful memories for individual members. Care and understanding and perhaps a change of subject may sometimes be necessary.

In planning future programmes of topics and ideas, avoid being too specific because role play should arise from the interests and experience of the members of the group. It is not difficult to stimulate a flow of thoughts through discussions on familiar situations, topical events, the problems of daily living and the links of these matters with each person's past.

Topics to explore

- Family situations and events: births, school, teenage years, weddings and funerals.

- Relationships – their importance, values and problems.

- The good old days.

- Work, holidays, travel.

Use newspapers, books, poetry and music – all can be sources of ideas and reminders of the tapestry of time remembered.

Use props: make a collection of clothes, hats, scarves, shawls, wigs, umbrellas, sunshades, uniforms or anything else that comes to hand to use if they help the imagination and the action.

Playing to an audience

In spite of the introductory advice that role play is best not performed as entertainment for an audience, there is always the possibility that there may be a request for this to be done. The wish to do this may even come from the group itself. If it is considered that they are confident enough, arrange a short performance of any scenes that they choose and that are suitable. But observe these rules:

- Do not hold extensive rehearsals.

- Show it as role play – informal and unscripted.

- Stand by to support any who experience stage nerves or memory lapses.

11

Reminiscence

At its simplest level, reminiscence is part of our daily conversation. We talk about what we did last night, last week, on holiday, when we were teenagers or children. The past is our life.

Reminiscence for the elderly in a care home is often at this simple level, as it is for everybody else in daily exchanges with other people. It is only when it is used in a structured activity that it takes on different aspects and offers interesting developments.

The value of reminiscence

- It is a natural activity that requires no skills for a person to take part in.

- Coming into a care home can be a traumatic experience. Reminiscence helps a person get to know other residents with similar problems and to form new relationships.

- It helps staff in making assessments to know the life history and the potential abilities of each resident.

- It can provide support to a resident for the memory of any loss or grief in the past.

- It can be enjoyable and interesting and encourage self-confidence in a resident.

Reminiscence as an activity

Although reminiscence will often be used on a one-to-one basis in informal conversation, it is especially useful as a group activity. It can provide a wide variety of themes for exploring the past. Exchanging memories of familiar topics with others can be stimulating and encourage less vocal residents to take part.

Reminiscence is not a difficult activity, but it needs careful preparation and a lively leader to make it interesting. In planning a programme, it is best to choose a series of themes that can be linked and provide a natural progression. As reminiscence is concerned with the events and experiences of people's lives there are an abundance of interesting topics within each theme to explore and talk about. Examples include:

- childhood

- schooldays

- home life

- family and friends

- work

- wartime.

Each theme can provide various topics that are likely to cover many of the main experiences in people's lives. Once a group has been established, its members should discuss which theme they would like to follow. It is important to provide structure to each session so that it deals with one particular topic at a time. There will often be some overlapping, but without direction the programme will become formless and in danger of repetition.

Examples of topics within a theme include the following list for the theme of 'childhood':

- toys
- games
- clothes
- brothers, sisters or friends
- bedtimes
- nursery rhymes
- fears
- food and sweets.

There is nothing definitive about such a list. It should be made after a discussion with the group members as to which topics they would like to talk about. Be flexible – it is their past, not yours. Decide on the number of sessions you expect to hold, with provision for extending them or starting another theme.

Collecting triggers

A topic is best approached and supported through various triggers that are likely to evoke memories. These may be visual, listening to specific sounds or music, or using touch or smell.

Making a collection of items from the past is interesting and revealing. Invite members of the group or their families to make contributions if they are willing to do so. You need their photographs – of residents as children and teenagers and of special occasions as they grew older. You may be given reminders of the past such as old newspapers or magazines, comics, theatre programmes and sports events. Cards and certificates can evoke memories: christening cards, wedding invitations, school reports, examination results, swimming certificates and perhaps wartime ration books.

Such personal mementos have the stamp of authenticity on them. They often have great significance for the person concerned and should be given care and respect. They make ideal material for reminiscence work, but you may need a filing system for storing them.

Less personal, but equally useful are pictures and articles of past scenes and events in the locality. Local newspapers often publish supplements with pictures and accounts of how a town has changed over the years. Such material may be copied, mounted and kept in plastic folders to prevent wear and tear. Local libraries have books with illustrations of the area in the past and, with permission, selections may be copied and, if necessary, enlarged. Many items such as old magazines, games and household articles from earlier times can often be found at jumble sales and market stalls.

If making collections is difficult, reminiscence boxes containing items, photographs and notes on particular topics can be hired or purchased. Details of distributors are listed at the end of the chapter.

Running a session

Have an assistant if possible: another staff member, a relative or a volunteer who is interested and who may have skills or knowledge that will help the session. Make sure you have a comfortable, quiet room with any necessary equipment.

Ensure everyone can see and hear each other so that there is a relaxed atmosphere.

There can be no specific way to run a group: have clear objectives, patience and some good humoured order. The main purpose is to encourage the members to talk and exchange their memories. Some will be keen to do so and may monopolise things at first while others will just listen. The leader may need to remind members that everyone should have the chance to speak and be heard. Rules of courtesy in a group are usually established quite easily.

The easiest way to start a session is with visual triggers – using photographs of people and places or a few objects to display or pass round. Don't have too many at one time as this can create confusion. Asking members to try to match the photographs of children with any of the members in the group can help to break the ice – if it exists. It is an easy step from this to discuss their memories of childhood. What is their very earliest memory? Who remembers being in a pram or pushchair? What other children or people are remembered the most clearly from those times?

A leader should decide whether it would be helpful to form small groups to look at separate items and talk about any specific aspect of the topic. This may be helpful for any quiet ones who may find it easier than in a large group, but there should be no pressure on anyone who does not wish to speak.

The group can be asked if they would like to make a record of their memories and perhaps create a scrapbook of pictures and short accounts of what they have done in the past.

Once a group is established, other topics can follow in similar fashion. Experience soon helps a leader to choose triggers that will provoke interest and discussion. There is a constant need, however, to be sensitive to anyone who may find some memories distressing. The past is not 'the good old days' for everyone and some memories can produce painful emotions. This is part of reminiscence work and it should be accepted as inevitable at times. It should not be ignored and it can be an occasion for other members to show sympathy and understanding for events they will recognise as familiar in their own lives.

Sounds

The use of different sounds can be especially evocative of a particular time or place. Some of the following sounds, which can be obtained from recordings, may be useful to be played when exploring a topic relevant to them:

- The ebb and flow of waves on a beach.
- Bird song, the cries of gulls, crows or owls.
- A dog barking, a cat howling, a baby crying.
- Sounds of farm animals – cows, sheep, horses.
- Bells – church, alarm clock, bicycle, door bell.
- Alarm sirens – ambulances, police cars, wartime.
- Trumpets, drums, bagpipes.
- The wind, thunder, rain.

Many of these and other sounds can be obtained from local libraries.

Music

Music can be a most effective means of reviving memories. However, if it is to be part of, or as a support to, a reminiscence topic it has to be chosen with care. It can be a distraction if it diverts memories on to a different course to the one being explored. It is best used when the subject is linked directly with familiar musical associations such as Christmas, the New Year, Easter, the seasons, weather, night and day, and wartime. There are probably items of music or songs for every experience in the universe, but there is a limit to what can be resourced. The simplest solution is to obtain a selection of recorded popular song collections and musical items covering different decades chosen from the 1920s to recent times. There are recordings of particular singers, musical shows, films and TV series. A list of suppliers is at the end of the chapter. For using music as the sole trigger, see Chapter 13 on music.

Smells and tastes

These are often associated with each other and either can be used to support a topic with reminders of the past. A collection of samples of different substances or liquids can be made in small bottles that can be passed round for people to identify and to talk about. Samples can include: coffee, vinegar, pepper, garlic, petrol, polish, perfumes, herbs and spices.

If you can find them, let the group have a taste from a selection of the sweets of long ago, such as acid drops, liquorice, sherbet dabs, bulls-eyes, gobstoppers and humbugs.

If there are facilities for a small group to do some cooking, suggest some ideas from childhood days: fairy cakes, flapjacks, gingerbread men, chocolate faces, Yo-Yo biscuits and jam tarts. (See Chapter 18 on cookery.)

If it is practical and safe, take a group to pick blackberries and turn the harvest into bramble jelly to be eaten on scones.

Some smells and tastes can't be stored, but they will probably be remembered from the impressions people had when they were young:

- Washing day – before the machine.

- Houses – furniture polish, mothballs, coal fires, tobacco, boiled cabbage.

- Shops – fishmongers, fried fish and chips, ironmongers, drapers, bakers, chemists.

- School – cloakrooms, classrooms, chemistry labs, swimming pool, school dinners.

- Countryside – grass cutting, hay making, farmyards, woods in autumn.

- Seaside – the shore, the sea, seaweed, seaside rock.

Continuity

Reminiscence can become an ongoing activity that is able to provide many opportunities for linked experiences throughout the year. These can be as simple or as extensive as is wished and according to the resources and time available. Occasions that can be considered include:

- the seasons

- festivals

- anniversaries

- fashions.

Further reading

Age Exchange publishes a whole range of handbooks on social conditions, leisure activities and wartime experiences from the first half of the 20th century. A list can be obtained from the Age Exchange Centre.

Two books on general reminiscence from Age Exchange are:

Bruce, E., Hodgson, S. and Schweitzer, P. (1999) *Reminiscing with People with Dementia*. London: Age Exchange.

This contains many ideas for people with or without dementia.

And:

Osborn, C. (1993) *The Reminiscence Handbook*. London: Age Exchange.

This is a practical 'how to do it' book with many creative ideas.

Age Exchange also stock reminiscence boxes for hire. Their contact details are:

Age Exchange
11 Blackheath Village
London SE3 9LA
Tel: 0208 318 9105
www.age-exchange.org.uk

Another useful book is:

Gibson, F. (1994) *Reminiscence and Recall*. London: Age Concern England.

This is a guide to good practice.

12

Everyday Occupations

These activities need no preparation, few resources and can contribute to the daily routine of the home. They concern the various simple tasks that can be done around the home by the residents. Before any doubts are raised as to this being a ploy to use free labour, it is a fact that residents often ask if they can do anything to help in the running of the home. They say that they miss doing the daily tasks they once did in their own home, and they would like to make a similar contribution to their present life. Any arrangements for residents to help in this way must be completely voluntary.

Some suggestions include:

- Helping to lay tables for meals.

- Clearing away after meals.

- Serving drinks or snacks.

- Arranging and tending flower displays.

- Delivering post to residents.

- Arranging displays of newspapers and magazines.

- Running a library. Choosing books for residents with limited mobility.

- Keeping a daily menu board.

- Reading to residents with poor sight.

- Exercising or tending pets.

- Helping frailer residents on walks in the garden or to local shops.

13

Music

Music should be an integral part of every care home's activities. Music makes a vital contribution to most people's lives in so many ways. Whether we listen to it by choice, incidentally from its part in entertainment or at ceremonies, or as an active player or singer, music is never far away.

Since early times music has been a constant accompaniment to human behaviour. For, as far back as can be traced, music has been used for entertainment, celebration, rituals and religious ceremonies. In many cultures, music has been used as a healing force to relieve the effects of illness and stress. In recent times this knowledge has led to the development of music therapy to help people with mental health problems, physical disabilities and the relief of depression and pain. The fact that such specialised uses of music are the responsibility of professionally trained therapists indicates that music is a powerful activity to use.

What does music do for people?

Music can:

- Stimulate the emotions through a range of feelings from the calm and relaxed to the exuberant and passionate.

- Affect bodily functions such as heart rate, blood pressure, respiration, and reduce the effects of pain, anxiety and stress.

- Evoke reminiscences of past life events and experiences.

- Aid communication of feelings and emotions to people who have few or no verbal abilities.

- Stimulate pleasurable activities: listening, singing, dancing, exercising, playing an instrument and using percussion instruments.

- Provide opportunities for visits to concerts, musical shows and local musical events in community centres, schools and colleges.

- Encourage people to socialise in the common enjoyment of music.

Precautions

However, despite all its advantages, music should be used with care in a mixed community. People's preferences for different forms of music can vary widely and if they are compelled to listen to a type they dislike this can cause extreme reactions. The playing of 'blanket' music constantly can be an irritant and an annoying distraction to some. The practice of some care workers of playing music while performing routine tasks in residential rooms can be a cause of tension if the music does not appeal.

Preparations

Before forming a group and arranging a programme, consider what resources are available and what is needed. If anyone on the staff or among the residents can play an instrument such as a piano, keyboard, accordion or guitar, and is prepared to perform, this will provide the appeal and impact that live music always brings. Often the main standby will be to rely on the use of audio equipment – a CD player. A selection of song sheets in large print should be collected even though it is unlikely that they will cover every eventuality.

Choosing music

Once a group has been formed, the first task must be to establish the main musical interests of the members. Collect their suggestions, their memories of what they would like to listen to, their favourite performers, singers and musical shows or films. Some are likely to have recordings of their own and will be pleased to share them with the group for future programmes.

In catering for a group that is likely to represent a cross-section of the public, the predominant choices are likely to be from the familiar popular music that they grew up with. Bearing in mind the different age groups, it is important to link the styles of the old with the new. Frank Sinatra did this and became one of the most popular singers of pre-rock popular music. Innumerable songs, singers, films, musicals, radio and TV programmes have provided a huge miscellany of memories and associations.

It will be impossible to cater for every particular choice. A general approach is to offer recordings of music from different decades, and collections of particular singers. Local libraries can often supply or obtain recordings. Old song books and sheet music can be an interesting source to provide a group with musical memories they would like to revive. If there are requests for jazz, classical, operatic or ballet music, decide whether there is sufficient demand for these forms to be included.

People with dementia

Music is particularly useful in communicating with and providing activities for people with dementia. Playing familiar music with marked rhythms for a small group to sing to or for dancing can be very successful. This needs a leader with empathy who can encourage them to take part in a common enjoyment of the music. It appears to penetrate their confusion and provide a recognisable link to hidden memories. Those with more advanced symptoms can also participate in musical activities. Even if they can only tap their feet, clap or move in time to the tempo, it is a sign of a recognised response.

Using percussion instruments

Joining in with music using simple percussion instruments can be an enjoyable activity. No particular skills are required. Percussion can be used with people of any ability. Research has shown that most people have the natural ability to imitate the rhythms they hear and can participate spontaneously when they are given the means to join in.

In the initial stages, a leader is needed to 'conduct' the actions, but this role can often be taken over by a member of the group. Play some recorded music with a marked rhythm – marches, country dances or waltzes. The percussion accompaniment is to maintain the rhythmic beat of the melody. Doing this is only an extension of when people tap their feet or hands in time to familiar music. It can be done by people at any level, if they are physically able, including those with dementia.

Percussion instruments can be anything simple that is capable of making sounds, such as:

- Pairs of short wooden sticks or claves that are stuck together to make a hollow beat. Claves can be cut from broom handles.

- Pairs of rolls of sandpaper with different grits. The ends need to be taped to prevent them unravelling and are used to make sounds by scraping them together.

- Shakers – made using plastic food cartons or tins containing a handful of dried peas or seeds.

Other easily played instruments can sometimes be found in car boot sales, jumble sales, junk shops and street markets, such as hand drums, table xylophones, gongs and triangles.

Activities

All sessions in which music is to be listened to should be enjoyable occasions. Try to obtain a quiet, comfortable room or area that has good auditory features with room for wheelchairs and where there are likely to be few interruptions. Aim for a maximum of no more than 12 in a group. Use a stereo system if possible, and make sure it is in good order with an output of at least 15 watts. Plan programmes that have variety. Keep them short and have a break for refreshments and some discussion or exchange or reminiscences about the music people have heard.

Plan programmes that are linked to particular themes

Examples include:

- music from different decades

- wartime music and songs

- songs from popular musical shows or films

- music from different countries.

When the group is well established invite them to plan and present some programmes of their own. Hold musical quizzes in which members have to identify the titles or origins of tunes or the names of singers. Invite musicians from local societies, schools or community centres to give live performances. Arrange a 'Desert Island Discs' programme for a member of the staff to choose a selection of favourite music to be played to an audience. Plan ahead to arrange special programmes to play to audiences for seasonal occasions.

A reference list of recorded music

The following is a selection of some of the most popular 'middle-of-the-road' music, composers, bands and singers from the last 70 years that are frequently asked for by older people, and which can be found on recordings and recent re-issues:

- Dance bands of the 1930s, 1940s and 1950s.

- Ballroom dance bands – Victor Sylvester; Latin American – Edmundo Ros; Mexican – Herb Alpert.

- Light music – Viennese waltzes – Strauss, Mantovani, Eric Coates, Henry Mancini, Roger Quilter.

- Operettas – Offenbach, Strauss family, Gilbert and Sullivan.

- Marches – Sousa, Vaughan Williams, Elgar.

- Musical plays – Ivor Novello, Noel Coward.

- Musical shows – *Show Boat, Oklahoma, South Pacific, Kiss Me Kate, The King and I, Singing in the Rain, West Side Story, Oliver!, The Sound of Music.*

- Composers – Cole Porter, Gershwin, Irving Berlin, Andrew Lloyd Webber.

- Groups – Beatles, Abba, Supremes, Bee Gees.

- Singers – Bing Crosby, Fred Astaire, Judy Garland, Louis Armstrong, Harry Belafonte, Doris Day, Frank Sinatra, Peggy Lee, Vera Lynn, Perry Como, Eva Cassidy, Tony Bennett, Tom Jones, Petula Clark, Julie Andrews, Dusty Springfield, Dionne Warwick, Diana Ross, Elaine Paige, Liza Minelli, Barbra Streisand, Simon and Garfunkel, Neil Diamond, Nana Mouskouri, Cliff Richard, David Essex, Robbie Williams.

- Country and Western and folk – Carter family, Woody Guthrie, Dolly Parton, Patsy Kline, John Denver, Gene Autry, Hank Williams, Jody Miller, Garth Brooks.

- Classical – classic FM collections, Lesley Garrett, Kiri Te Kanawa, Pavarotti, James Galway, John Williams.

- Piano – Scott Joplin, Oscar Peterson, Art Tatum.

14

Arts and Crafts

Any form of arts and crafts should be an enjoyable activity that is not just a time-filler, but one that encourages creativity and self-expression. This is not to expect artificial standards of achievement beyond the capabilities of residents. Activities need to be pitched at an appropriate level that does not depend on special skills or the learning of difficult techniques. At the same time it should be recognised that people, no matter what their age or experience, are capable of interesting and imaginative ideas. Give them the chance to experiment and offer them high ideals, not low expectations. Never stoop to providing 'painting by numbers' or expect them to colour in ready-made outlines. There is the added bonus that within an arts and crafts group people learn from each other and often develop an enjoyable sense of collaboration.

An activities organiser who has experience or interest in the subject will be able to select suitable activities from the vast choice available. Other staff, relatives or volunteers from the local community who have skills in any branch of the subject can be invited to help and advise. In addition there are many well-illustrated books in libraries that give expert guidance and information on different topics.

Precautions

In selecting activities consider the need for:

- Simplicity in operation.

- Materials – cost and ease of storage – supplies of paper, card, pencils, felt tip pens, brushes, plants and scissors.

- Resources – a suitable room with tables, sufficient space and illumination and time between meals if using the dining room.

Activities

Painting

Those who have had previous experience of painting in water colours or oils and wish to continue may only need ideas for subjects. Their imagination may be stimulated by a piece of music, a song, a poem or a story. The different seasons and the weather can often suggest ideas. A change of scenery from their everyday surroundings may be all they need to start a picture. Art outings should be in the programme. Borrow library books that suggest subjects and different techniques.

Collage

There are no rules or conventions to worry about in this craft. Make a collection of vivid pictures from magazines, colour supplements or travel brochures. Gather pieces of fabric, lace, velvet, net, ribbons, buttons and sequins. Basic equipment includes scissors, felt pens, firm card or hardboard for mounting, quick drying adhesive, brushes and cocktail sticks for spreading it.

Suggest a subject: be daring – like Picasso, Matisse and Braque – because anything goes – abstracts, faces, figures, animals, the sun, moon and stars, dream flowers. Build up a picture by cutting, tearing or overlapping the different materials. Arrange and rearrange until something emerges as it will surely do. Then glue it all to the base. (Local printers will often let you have out of stock supplies of card.)

Pressed flower pictures

This is an ancient craft that has been practised for centuries. It is inexpensive, and requires no particular skills apart from care, patience and an eye for design and arrangement. Liaise with members of the gardening group and ask them to grow some suitable flowers for pressing. Many common wild flowers can be picked from roadside verges and on common land, providing they are unprotected species such as buttercups, daisies, speedwell, celandine, cow parsley and silverweed. Trial and error will show which flowers, small ferns and grasses give the best results when pressed.

Pick flowers and foliage on a dry day and press them as soon as possible. Place them between sheets of newspaper or in the pages of old telephone directories, and weigh them down with anything heavy. Leave for a least a week or longer until the specimens are completely dry.

Arrange a picture before finally mounting the items on cartridge paper cut to the required size and in a shade that complements the tones of the flowers. Use tweezers and a fine paint brush to move and position them. Apply a small amount of adhesive with a cocktail stick to each item and apply gentle pressure to mount it. Give the finished picture a firm backing card before covering it with glass in a picture frame.

Small pictures can be made for greeting cards or calendars. These can be protected with clear self-adhesive film that needs special care in applying. This is a rewarding craft that teaches a person how to be artistic and imaginative though the natural beauty of the subject.

Printmaking
PATTERNS AND PICTURES FROM PRINTS
This is an interesting and creative craft that requires no special skills apart from care and imagination. Prints can be produced using simple, everyday equipment without the use of a printing press.

What is needed:

- a rigid, smooth base about 30 cm × 25 cm (12 inches × 10 inches) – such as a formica-covered board or a clean metal tray

- a supply of soft absorbent paper to print on

- paints – poster, acrylic or water-based ink

- brushes, a rubber roller, a sponge pad

- a craft knife

- felt tip pens

- masking tape

- different sized spoons for burnishing

- newspapers for covering tables

- cleaning rags.

Patterns and images can be produced from a large variety of items that can be used as printers, as long as each has at least one flat surface. Some examples include coins, bottle lids, corks, the base of pots, keys, buttons, dried leaves, stones, bark and driftwood. Printers can be made out of blocks of wood with thread or string wound round them. Other useful sources are the cut surfaces of some vegetables and fruit: potatoes, turnips, carrots, swedes and apples can be carved to leave a raised shape on the surface.

When a printer or printers have been selected, colour is then applied to their surfaces – using poster paint, acrylic, or printing ink – and a test print is made. The colour medium can be applied with a paint brush, a sponge, a roller or a sponge pad. The printer is then laid paint side down on the paper and given hand pressure and removed carefully to avoid smudging the print. Another method is to place the paper over the painted printer and, holding the paper firmly, rub a spoon over the area on the back of the paper to be printed.

There are plenty of opportunities to experiment:

- print one colour on top of another

- print one print on top of another

- add brush strokes around or between blocks of prints

- make printers by cutting shapes out of card, corrugated cardboard or sandpaper.

Printing does not have to be confined to creating patterns. There is no limit to the subjects it can be used for. Pictures can be built up to create such images as people's faces, animals, birds, fishes, reptiles and dragons. A wash of colours can provide the background of a landscape of sky, hills, mountains or sea on which features can be printed such as the sun, moon, stars, houses, ships or trees.

Printmaking is capable of creating unique images strikingly different from the results of traditional painting and without the need for the technical skills that painting requires.

Salt dough modelling

This can be used in the same way as clay, but supplies to make it are at hand in every kitchen. The recipe is:

- 2 cups of plain flour
- 1 cup of cooking salt
- three-quarters cup of water
- 2 cups of cooking oil.

The size of cup doesn't matter as long as the proportions are observed! Mix all the ingredients and knead for about 10 minutes (or use a food mixer with a dough hook) into a workable dough. It can be given general colour at this stage by blending paint into it, or separate batches can be given different colours for particular items. Make the models within a few hours to get the best results.

Start modelling simple flat items for practice: different shaped leaves, flat fish, starfish, a half moon, stars. Progress to shells, flowers, plaited garlands, shallow bowls, animals, birds and faces. Where there is a need, separate items can be stuck together with water. The surface of an item can be textured with such simple tools as a fork, a comb or a cocktail stick. Embellishments, such as seed heads, twigs, small shells or stones, and peppercorns, can be wetted and pressed into the dough. The finished models need slow baking on a greased baking tray. When thoroughly dry and cooled, they can be painted. This will usually require practice on unwanted pieces of baked dough to achieve the effects that may be required. Finally, give the models a coat of varnish.

Mosaics

Mosaic-making has been practised to great effects since early times, as can be seen in the remains of beautiful decorations found in Italy, Greece and Egypt. The principles of making mosaic pictures are easily mastered today, and simple devices can now be used to produce attractive designs and projects. It is work that requires care and patience and it suits the slow tempo of people who are not in a hurry.

Avoid mosaic kits, which are usually expensive and which supply ready-made designs that do not encourage creativity. The simplest method is to use a design grid, which is a plastic honeycomb of small, square shallow depressions for easily arranging the tiles. The cheapest tiles are ceramic and these can be bought glazed or unglazed in loose mixtures of colours.

A design or shape such as a flower, a fish or a bird is drawn or copied onto a large sheet of paper cut to the required size. The design grid is placed over it, a section at a time, and its position marked. The tiles are then filled in to the grid squares in the chosen colours to make the part of the design it covers. Where the shape demands it, individual tiles will need to be cut using mosaic cutters that are simple to use. Each completed grid section of tiles is then fixed together by pressing gummed paper over it. This is then transferred to a plywood base and cemented in place. When secure the gummer paper is washed off each section, and the complete design is grouted. If it is to be used as a picture, a framed edge can be provided, and hanging plates fixed to the back. Details giving suppliers of mosaic materials, accessories and books on the subject are given at the end of this chapter.

Photography

A photographic group can provide interesting activities that are easy to arrange and the results can supply the home with a continuous record of its community life. Modern compact cameras are simple to use and films are capable of producing good colour prints taken in and out of doors. Digital cameras allow for experimentation with different techniques and settings as photographs may be viewed as soon as they are taken, allowing the photographer to choose only successful shots for developing. However, these cameras can be small and fiddly to use so may be unsuitable for those who do not feel at home with electronic devices or those with poor eyesight. The home may own its own camera, but it is likely that some residents will have one of their own.

The group should decide on an allocation of their different activities to be carried out by different members: those who will take the photographs (which can include wheelchair users); those who will arrange the time and place of the venues; and others who will organise the results, with captions for mounted displays and eventual storage of the photographs in loose leaf albums with clear plastic pages.

Apart from recording special occasions and seasonal events, it is worth suggesting projects that give purpose to the continuing activities of the group. A series of features could be made on topics such as:

- A day in the life of... – showing the work of individual members of the staff – the manager, a nurse, a care assistant, the cook and the gardener.

- Other activities in the home – in arts and crafts, gardening, cooking, games.

- The gardens through the seasons, from spring to winter.

- The local town or village – its shops, churches, pubs, community centre, library and people of note.

- The tradespeople who call at the home.

PICTURE-MAKING ADVICE

- Take pictures of people doing things rather than arranging static poses or groups. Some people dislike having their photograph taken, and spontaneous 'candid' pictures are often better.

- Get in close whenever possible.

- Avoid camera shake: stand firmly, or sit down or lean so that photographs are sharp and unblurred.

- For indoor photographs use a fast film – 400 ASA – and make sure the camera has a flash.

Other crafts

There are numerous other handicrafts that individuals or groups may like to take up, such as: stencilling, rubber stamp printing, silk painting, painting on glass and ceramic objects, needlecrafts, crochet, patchwork and tapestry. Libraries usually have many books with practical suggestion on these subjects.

Further reading

Painting

Gair, A. and Sideway, I. (2005) *How to Paint.* London: New Holland Publishers.

West, K. (1993) *How to Draw and Paint Wild Flowers.* London: Herbert Press.

Collage

Michel, K. (2005) *The Complete Guide to Altered Imagery: Mixed Techniques for Collage.* Beverly, MA: Quarry Books.

Pressed flower pictures

Black, P. (1998) *The Complete Book of Pressed Flowers.* London: Dorling Kindersley.

Printing

Desmet, A. and Anderson, J. (2000) *Handmade Prints.* London: A&C Black.

Creative printmaking without a press.

Salt dough modelling

Tilley, J. and Welby, S. (1995) *The Dough Craft Sourcebook.* London: Hamlyn.

Mosiacs

Baird, H. (1997) *Mosaics.* London: Lorenz Books/Anness Publishing.

Cheek, M. (1997) *Mosaics in a Weekend.* London: New Holland Publishers.

Goodwin, E.M. (1996) *Decorative Mosaics.* London: New Holland Publishers.

SUPPLIERS

Paul Fricker Ltd
452 Pinhoe Road
Exeter
Devon
EX4 8HN

Caesar Ceramics
358 Edgware Road
London
W2 1EB

Edgar Udney & Co Ltd
The Mosaic Centre
314 Balham High Road
London
SW17 7AA

Reed Harris Ltd
Riverside House
Carnwath Road
London
SW6 3HS

Photography

Frost, L. (2003) *The Creative Photography Handbook*. Newton Abbot, Devon: David & Charles.

15

Discussions and Debates

A discussion group might appear to be a simple and easily run activity. In fact, it can prove to be quite difficult, and it requires careful preparation and use of various strategies if it is to succeed. Many elderly people find it difficult to express opinions or make comments in formal discussions. It requires a confidence to do this, which causes many to be hesitant. Another problem is the tendency of older people to have set opinions, which makes it difficult for them to be impartial when discussing controversial topics.

Is it worth attempting? Of course, but it needs to be presented in ways that will extend the notion of a friendly chat among the group to a form of organised discussion. What are the aims?: to encourage the free expression of ideas, to allow opinions to be aired and to listen and consider the views of other people.

Preparations

Start by choosing a title for the activity that avoids the somewhat forbidding title of 'discussions'. Here are some suggestions:

- Points of view.

- What do you think?

- Views on the news.

- Talking points.

- Questions of the day.

The leader of such a group needs to be articulate, astute and unbiased. Personal views have to be suppressed and encouragement given to anyone ready to speak. If it is lonely out there, have a partner for support, and work together to a plan that produces an exchange of views and, it is to be hoped, a lively debate.

As a beginning, it is useful to break up the group into smaller units with no more than four or five in each, and containing a confident speaker as the leader. This creates a closer, more friendly circle that encourages conversation. Provide a clearly stated topic on a flip chart, with some leading suggestions to follow. After a reasonable period ask for feedback from each unit leader, and if this provides interesting ideas or dissent, a wider discussion among the whole group can develop.

It will probably be necessary to continue with this more intimate form of grouping for several sessions. There is no disadvantage in this if it achieves the main purpose of creating the experience for everyone of being part of the give and take of debate.

Developing topics

Presenting a topic can be given a greater impact or stimulate different ideas by using various methods. The following are some that have proved to be successful:

- Collect and display the headlines from various newspapers that show diverse views on the same topic. Talk about the part played by the media in influencing public opinion.

- Present a topic, with the leader and an assistant giving opposing views on a controversial subject, such as immigration, public transport, fear of crime, standards in TV programmes, working mothers.

- Record the beginning or part of a discussion programme from radio or TV. 'Call-in' programmes are frequently presented on radio, when listeners telephone, text or email opinions on topics of the day.

Discussions need not be controversial. There is much to be explored in debating ideas, opinions and judgements on many of the subjects that occur in everyday life. The following examples could be considered:

- Where is the best place to live – village, town, city, housing estate, high-rise flats, countryside, seaside, north or south?

- What are the best qualities in a person – honesty, generosity, patience, tolerance, sense of humour?

- What makes you angry, embarrassed, amused, frightened?

- Which celebrity do you most admire – and why?

- Which is the most important job – doctor, nurse, teacher, police officer, member of the armed forces?

- What do you think of advertisements, gambling, pets, the young today?

- What superstitions do you have?

- What if – cars and planes had never been invented, you could live to 150, Hitler had defeated Britain, there could be time travel to the past or future, life is discovered on another planet?

Newsletters

Every care home should produce its own newsletter. It can be the voice of the home, linking the residents with each other, the staff, relatives and the local community. A newsletter helps to show the quality of the home's overall care as seen in its opportunities for social, cultural and leisure activities. It should reflect the interests, opinion and ideas of the residents and provide them with some fun and enjoyment. A newsletter does not take the place of a home's information brochure for prospective residents, but it can be a valuable adjunct. It can also be a useful aid for gaining outside support for projects and events.

Why then are there only a minority of homes that produce a newsletter on a regular basis? The usual reasons given are the amount of work it entails, and the lack of sufficient 'news'. Both these problems can be resolved. It should certainly not be the sole responsibility of the activities organiser to produce a newsletter even though that person should take the lead. A small group of interested residents could undertake the task, aided by relatives and anyone in the locality with a computer.

Form an editorial group

Collect a selection of newspapers – dailies, tabloids, broadsheets, Sunday and local. Pass them round and discuss what features could be adapted to provide ideas for inclusion. A preliminary list might comprise:

- items of news about the home and the residents
- articles by residents and others
- opinions on current affairs
- interviews
- reviews of TV, films, books and music
- stories and poems
- letters to the editor
- miscellaneous – puzzles, word games, crosswords, competitions, jokes.

Produce a poster outlining what is required.

Poetry and verse

Poetry? Who reads poetry? If that sounds like a challenge, then why not try the experiment of using poetry as an activity? You need to like the idea and to enjoy poetry yourself, but you don't have to be an expert or very knowledgeable about it as there are many resources you can use.

Poetry is likely to be a new experience for most residents. Many will not have read or listened to poetry since they left school. The memory of poetry will probably be limited to nursery rhymes and some of the classic poems they had to study when young. Poetry had a bad reputation in the past as being difficult and obscure. This was mainly the result of expecting school children to understand poems intended for adults, and often on subjects that held little interest for them. Thankfully, poetry is now regarded as a far more enjoyable and popular form of literature.

Young people today are introduced to a poetry that speaks directly to their experiences in a language they can understand. They are encouraged to write their own verse in free, expressive forms that are often used by modern poets.

This new approach to poetry has been taken up in many quarters. It has reached the hoardings, the pubs, the London Underground. Public readings of poetry have become a regular feature, with groups of poets reading their work in schools, colleges, community centres, libraries and at poetry festivals. Their poems are often short, sharp, funny or painful and deal with everyday subjects from football to food and family problems.

The BBC regularly broadcasts poetry programmes dealing with every type of poetry from traditional to modern styles. It has run a number of polls for its listeners to vote for their favourites. The results of these have been published in a series of books and recordings on cassette tapes and CDs with such titles as *The Nation's Favourite Poems*. Details of these and other resources are at the end of the chapter.

With something like a ready-made programme available, running a poetry group is a feasible and enjoyable possibility. Listening to poetry well read is the key to winning people over to its attractions. The groups of poems often linked to a theme in many of these anthologies and recordings make it easy to choose a topic to use. Hearing or reading poems will often awaken memories of others, and this can lead to discussion and perhaps the making of a group anthology or favourite title.

Most modern anthologies offer a wide scope of poems that may range from familiar ones in traditional forms to the works of modern writers. There are interesting collections that cater for a range of interests. Some are devoted to women's interests and opinions, the Second World War, animals, and a recent one has the optimistic subtitle of *101*

Happy Poems. As well as these there are collections of comic poems and nonsense verse. Titles of some of these are listed at the end of the chapter.

Activities

Different activities should be planned to provide variety and ongoing interest in the various forms of poetry.

Individual poets

Collect, read and listen to the different poems of one poet. There are recordings of the works of the well-known poets and many libraries have separate poetry collections. Apart from the traditional classics, consider any of the following:

- Charles Causley
- Ted Hughes
- Elizabeth Jennings
- W.H. Auden
- Robert Frost
- Christina Rossetti.

Some of the modern poets who have written about everyday subjects and who usually make poetry relevant and humorous or sardonic are:

- Philip Larkin
- Roger McGough
- Carol Ann Duffy
- Gareth Owen
- Brian Patten

- Kit Wright
- Wendy Cope
- Liz Lochhead.

Poem for the week

The group could discuss different types of poems from which once poem could be chosen to be used each week as a focal point. Each poem chosen could be copied onto a poster and either illustrated appropriately or decorated with patterns. Obtain a permanent display board for residents and staff to see and read the poems on display. The subject could cover the seasons, local and national events, memories, opinions, humour and nonsense verse.

Writing verse

There may be some members in a group who have the talent and even the experience of writing poems in the traditional metred form that rhymes, but this is unlikely to apply to many. It is not easy to rhyme well. The attempt to rhyme can cause unsuitable expressions to be used that spoil the effect of the poem. The best approach is through free verse.

Free verse

Free verse has no conventional metre and using rhyme is a matter of choice. It may use lines of different length and is similar to the natural cadences of speech. Free verse has a long history going back to Shakespeare, Browning, Wordsworth and D.H. Lawrence. Here is a poem in free verse I wrote when my daughter was born:

1947

47 was a very cold year
The snow was high
When you first saw the light
Of life…

No need for you to know
Of winter's cold
And when I bent
To see your face
Your breath was warm

47 was a very cold year
You did not know –
How could you know,
That I had trudged
Through drifts of snow
To look upon your
Newborn face –
And find your breath
Was warm?

This is not a proposal for a creative writing course for the elderly. A poem or a piece of verse is not necessarily better than a letter, a notice, an essay or even an email – but it is different. It should look different and sound different. And while there is no need to go into complex processes on how to write a poem, there are some simple techniques that can help to prompt the creative means of achieving this.

WRITING GAMES

Give the group a word, a phrase or a sentence that they must copy, such as:

- Danger.
- Too late.

- I've lost it.

- Where have you been?

- I saw it happen.

- Nobody spoke.

- The door was locked.

As soon as they have written the starter, they must continue writing without a pause. They can write about anything – in any way they like. There should be no attempt to rhyme or to produce the shape of a poem. The simple aim is that writing words stimulates more words. Writing sentences creates more sentences. This removes inhibitions about what to write or how to write. Give a time limit – 10 minutes at the most. Then get them to edit what they have written and to try to write some of it as a piece of free verse. The results may vary from the interesting to the worthless, but it is the practice that is important in releasing the power of self-expression. With repeated sessions this device can produce positive results.

Another starting point is to give the first line of a poem. Residents have to continue in any way they choose, but without spending any time on trying to rhyme. Some examples could be:

- The wind was a torrent of darkness…

- As the sun went down…

- They said the house was haunted…

- It will not always be like this…

- Lie in the dark and listen…

Sometimes the rhythm of the words in the given line may suggest continuing in a similar style – a positive progression in the making of verse.

PICTURES

Make a collection of pictures – news photographs from newspapers, colour supplements, advertisements and different brochures. Put groups of five or six pictures into separate envelopes and make the mix as unrelated and dissimilar as possible. Each member has then to write in the same free way about the group of pictures they receive.

OBJECTS

Place on a large tray a group of objects that will provoke a train of ideas, such as a diary, a necklace, a glove, a doll, a key. Cover the articles with a cloth. When everybody is ready, remove the covering; then they must start to write immediately.

SOUNDS AND MUSIC

Obtain recorded sounds from a library. Choose one that creates a story, or provides reminders of a particular event: the sound of a distant train, a horse trotting, church bells, a plane taking off and so on. Play a short piece of music that suggests different moods – martial, the sea, mysterious.

These devices all create ideas and trigger the process of writing freely. Often this will result in a collection of disparate words and phrases. No matter; the collection is likely to contain thoughts, impressions and perhaps strong feelings, all of which are ingredients for a piece of verse or a real poem.

The editing of a free writing session should not be hurried. It requires consideration, careful selection, and probably lots of chopping and changing until a satisfactory result is achieved. There can be shared help and advice between the group members if they wish it. Reading work out to the group must be a personal choice and nobody must feel pressured to do so, or pushed to criticise the work of others. Generally there is a good spirit of cooperation among people who attempt this. Like all creative activities, the writing of poetry is likely to improve with practice and with the enjoyment of the challenge and the success it can often bring.

References

Agar, K. (*1947*) Unpublished poem.

Resource: Anthologies and recordings

Albery, N. (1994) *Poem for the Day*. London: Chatto.

Benson, G. (ed.) (2001) *Poems on the Underground*. 10th edition. London: Cassell.

Briers, R. (foreword) (1999) *The Nation's Favourite Shakespeare*. (1998) London: BBC Books.

Cope, W. (compiler) (2001) *Heaven on Earth: 101 Happy Poems*. *London: Faber & Faber*.

Dent, J.M. (selection) (2003) *More Poetry Please*. London: Phoenix.

Goodwin, D. (compiler) (1997) *The Nation's Favourite Love Poems*. London: BBC Books.

Heaney, S. and Hughes, T. (eds) (1982) *The Rattle Bag*. London: Faber & Faber.

(If you want just one anthology this would make an excellent choice. A wonderful book to dip into and every dip likely to please. From Shakespeare to Adrian Mitchell.)

Jones, G.R. (foreword) (1996) *The Nation's Favourite Poems*. London: BBC Books.

Jones, G.R. (ed.) (1998) *The Nation's Favourite Comic Poems*. London: BBC Books.

Lyttelton, H. (ed.) (1998) *Limericks – I'm Sorry I Haven't a Clue (team)*. London: Orion.

McGough, R. (1990) *Blazing Fruit. Selected Poems*. Harmondsworth: Penguin.

McLoughlin, P. (ed.) (1996) *Woman's Hour 50th Anniversary Poetry Collection*. Harmondsworth: Penguin/BBC.

Roberts, S. (ed.) (1993) *Poetry Please*. (Books of Favourite Poems: A Further Selection of Popular Poems from the Radio 4 Series). London: BBC Books.

Warwick, A. (ed. and compiler) (2000) *The Nation's Favourite Poems of Childhood*. London: BBC Books.

16

A Miscellany of Informal Activities

It is useful to have ready a prepared stock of easily arranged activities that can provide entertainment, competitive efforts or various games for short sessions and when longer items on the programme are not possible. Some residents may prefer taking part in these instead of being committed to regular attendance at major activities.

Quizzes

There is always a great abundance of quizzes available: in paperback books and in magazines and newspapers, which often provide lists of questions on particular topics. Care is needed to ensure that the questions are suitable and not too difficult. There can be competitions between groups or teams. 'Trivial Pursuit' is a popular game that caters for up to 36 players.

Inviting residents to make up a set of their own questions can be interesting. By delving into their past memories, asking questions about local people, places and events, a quiz can create an individual appeal of its own.

Brains trust

Inviting a group of people to form a panel to discuss their opinions on everyday topics can be entertaining and often illuminating. The panel can be made up of confident residents, relations or people from the locality to form a cross-section of people with particular experiences and views, such as a teacher, shopkeeper, librarian, policeman, farmer or anyone else who is willing to participate

Indoor games

The playing of indoor games has largely gone out of fashion since TV has taken over. The enjoyment that games once provided has been lost in the passive acceptance of ready-made entertainment. It is worth offering a selection of games that will recapture what was once a common leisure activity and provide some alternatives for bingo, which is often the only group game. Some suggestions include:

- Carpet bowls.

- Skittles.

- Quoits.

- Board games – draughts, chess, dominoes, backgammon, bagatelle, scrabble.

- Pencil and paper games – noughts and crosses, word squares.

- Card games – whist, rummy, cribbage, Newmarket, patience.

What's my job?

One person volunteers at a time to be questioned about the work they once did, or a job that they have chosen to imagine. The group take it in turns to ask questions about the work which can only be answered by 'yes' or 'no'. A limit of 20 questions is the usual allowance.

Memory games

Deterioration in memory affects most people as they get older. Most memory loss is short term and may only concern difficulty in recalling names and recent events and the need to remember everyday routines. Long-term memory is often retained and may be perfect for recollecting much of a person's past life. The most acute problems will be found in people with developing dementia, who may be unable to take part in recalling memories with any accuracy.

While many people rely on memory aids through notice boards, diaries, calendars, labels and daily lists, taking part in simple games that prompt the memory can be useful and enjoyable.

Kim's game

Collect a number of everyday items – 10–20 according to the abilities of the group. Put the items on a tray and cover them with a cloth. Place the tray on the floor or a low table. Suggest that the members use a method of remembering the items when they see them: to make up a story that links them; arrange them in groups according to size, colour or shape; form a series of initial letters of their names. When the group is ready, remove the cloth and give everyone 2–3 minutes to see and remember what is on the tray. Then cover the tray and ask everyone to write down as many of the items as they can remember. Ask the winner, the person who remembers the most items, to explain the system that they used.

Alphabet names

Sit the group in a circle. Either the leader or a resident stands in the centre and throws a soft ball to one of the circle and calls out a letter (avoiding difficult ones such as Q, X or Z). The person who catches the ball has to call out immediately five things beginning with the chosen letter. If successful, this person takes the place of the one in the centre. Variations can be made by choosing special categories such as towns, countries, flowers and so on beginning with the chosen letter.

Name the face

Make a collection of large pictures of people who are not well known, using photographs cut out of magazines. Paste the pictures on cards and number them. On separate cards write imaginary names – either first names or full names. Write the number of the picture on the back of the name card. Place the pictures with their name cards below them on a table or the floor. Give the group a few minutes to study the pictures and their names, then take the names away. Everyone must now try to name the faces.

Alibis

Two volunteers are sent out of the room. They have to plan where they were during a few hours on a certain day when an imaginary crime was committed. Each returns on their own.

The first person sits in the centre and is asked to describe where they were together during a period of several hours covering the time of the imaginary crime. Members take it in turn to ask the person a question on how they spent their time. Then the second person is brought in and questioned in the same way. If the two accounts are identical, they win. If there are three or more discrepancies, they are found guilty!

What was in the picture?

Display a large, clear picture mounted on a piece of card. Make sure it can be seen clearly by everyone. Tell them to look at all the details and try and remember them. After a few minutes remove the picture and give a prepared list of questions about the details in the picture to which they have to write the answers.

Memories

Compile a list of subjects that are likely to evoke memories. Have the group sit in a circle. Call out one of the subjects and ask the first of the group to say what this brings to mind. Proceed to the next person and continue around the circle. Some suggestions are:

- Christmas, Easter, autumn, winter
- summer holidays
- a circus
- a pantomime
- a school playground
- football

- an aeroplane trip
- sandcastles.

Some subjects may provoke general discussion and this should be encouraged to stimulate individual memories of past experiences.

Celebrities

Either prepare a list of well-known people from the past or present, or ask the group to choose three of their own and write them on slips of paper and put them in a container. Arrange the group in a circle, take out one slip at a time and ask each person in turn to name three facts about the person named. Suggestions include:

- The Duke of Windsor
- Judy Garland
- Vera Lynn
- Harold Macmillan
- Jeffrey Archer
- Margaret Thatcher
- John F. Kennedy.

17

ardening

Gardening can have special significance for care home residents. For many it is a familiar activity that they have practised in the past, and giving them the opportunity to take part in it again can boost their confidence. Gardening provides a change from their everyday surroundings, is a source of exercise in the fresh air and can help to maintain and often improve mobility.

However, a most important aspect of gardening for residents is to make it as easy as possible for them. It must be made an enjoyable activity, since if it is going to be a hard slog there won't be many volunteers! Traditional gardening requires residents who are mobile enough to bend, kneel, plant and stand up on their own. There is a better and easier way though: container gardening.

Container gardening

This is the easy alternative to the hard slog. The results can often be better than growing plants in open borders or beds, and containers are capable of providing spectacular displays. In recent years there has been a revolution in this method of growing plants. The increase in patios and paved areas in gardens and apartments with balconies has encouraged the widespread use of containers. It is an ideal way of gardening for people who are less mobile.

Advantages

- small planting area

- plants are easier to reach

- no digging and little weeding

- containers can be moved around to provide a changing display

- fewer attacks by slugs

- trailing plants are idea for containers

- tender plants can be protected indoors in winter.

The choice of containers

Garden centres and hardware stores stock large selections of containers in many different shapes, sizes, colours and materials. Suitable receptacles can often be found among discarded items in markets, country fairs and car boot sales. Old chimney pots, farm troughs, half barrels, old sinks and redundant wooden wheelbarrows all make attractive containers. Any receptacle can be used as long as it retains water and has sufficient depth for roots to develop and support plants. Drainage holes are needed in the base.

Collect an assortment of different sizes, heights and colours. The questions of which are the most suitable and where each is to go will be subjects to be discussed by the group later. Containers can be put anywhere that is appropriate in the available spaces: on patios, beside entrances and on paths or steps, if these are wide enough to allow unhindered passage. They can be placed in groups, or large ones can be used as focal points with special individual plants on display.

Containers include window boxes, hanging boxes and plastic pouches that can be hung anywhere. Other devices are raised beds made with bricks, building blocks or old railway sleepers; and even two or three old tyres placed on top of each other.

Starting a gardening group

While some gardening know-how is an advantage for an organiser, there is a wealth of information to be found in magazines, books, radio, TV and at garden centres. Apart from knowledgeable residents, there may be relatives who will be pleased to help and advise.

There is much preparation for members of a group to discuss and consider. If this is done during the winter, activities can get off to a good start in the spring. Planning can include:

- obtaining a range of containers

- choosing suitable positions and grouping

- using catalogues to choose seeds, plants and bulbs

- obtaining plants – getting contributions from local gardens, relatives, possible discounts from a garden centre

- indoor activities – seed sowing, cuttings, indoor containers

- vegetable growing

- sharing the work of sowing, potting, planting and tending.

The choice of plants

Permanent

Avoid any that will grow too large. Suitable types include hostas, patio roses, agapanthus, cordylines, phormiums.

Bedding plants

Most need planting every year. These are the mainstay of colourful displays from spring and early summer to autumn. Most of the following have trailing varieties: geraniums, fuchsias, begonias, impatiens, petunias, nasturtiums.

Bulbs

Apart from bulbs planted in autumn for the following spring, others that flower in the summer include gladioli, lilies, anemones, montbretia and freesias.

Vegetables

Some are best grown in grow-bags. Those that can be grown in containers include cherry tomatoes, dwarf runner beans and French beans, cucumbers and peppers. Strawberries also grow well in pots.

Herbs

Many herbs have attractive flowers as well as aromatic leaves. They can be grown in special terracotta pots with holes in the sides, or grown together in a tub or trough. Some of the best include parsley, chives, marjoram, tarragon and sage. Some can be brought indoors for the winter.

Planting in containers

Use a good quality compost – preferably a peat-free mixture, coir or John Innes No. 2 or No. 3. Plant firmly at the same depth as in the original pots. Water well and regularly thereafter. Either use slow release fertiliser pellets in the compost or feed regularly with a high potash liquid feed.

A mini-pond

On a smaller scale, a mini-pond in a container has similar attractions to an ordinary garden pond, but is quite easy to create. A large leakproof container is needed about 2 feet (60 cm) wide and deep enough to hold some 6–8 gallons (approx. 27–36 litres) of water. A half barrel in good condition would be suitable after painting the interior with a coating or bitumen. Another possibility is a second-hand fibreglass tank once used for storing water in a house loft.

A dwarf lily planted in a hessian-lined bucket can be lowered into the centre of the container and two or three marginal plants placed around the edges standing on bricks or similar supports. An oxygenating plant will make it possible to introduce a pair of goldfish.

Precautions and facilities

Outdoor gardening of any type requires precautions to ensure that the various activities are safe. Risk assessments of the medical conditions and mobility of participants must be a priority.

Access to all areas should be checked and made safe if necessary for any residents with disabilities or for wheelchair users. There should be convenient seats or resting places and handrails for steps or slopes.

Water supplies and storage facilities for garden tools and equipment should be easily accessible. A supply of light garden tools with long handles should be available as well as protective garden gloves.

Indoor gardening

If there is no greenhouse or conservatory, a suitable room will be needed with tables that can be covered and the area cleaned easily. Here activities such as planting bulbs, taking cuttings and seed sowing can be done. Growing some plants from seeds can have its difficulties. Tiny seeds are difficult to sow evenly, and emerging seedlings need special care and attention if they are to develop into strong plants. Seeds that are usually successful include sweet peas, lupins, nasturtiums, runner beans and French beans.

Indoor displays

Indoor house plants look and grow better when they are planted together in a group rather than in separate individual pots. These can make attractive projects for individuals or small groups to put together and tend. A container is needed that is large enough to hold several small or medium indoor plants. There is a large range of different sizes, shapes and leaf colours to choose from according to the arrangement that is planned.

Cover the base of the container with a layer of fine gravel and then fill with dampened potting compost and firm down. Choose plants that provide a variety of heights, leaf shapes and colours. Avoid any that will overspread the other plants. An example of a group might consist of a feather palm, a rex begonia, a coleus, and an ivy to trail over the edge.

Leave the plants in their pots and insert them into the compost so that this encloses each pot up to its rim. Keep the compost damp as this creates a humid atmosphere and a moist rooting base. Plants grow well together in these conditions. Water sparingly with a liquid feed regularly in spring and summer, but less so in winter. Keep in a good light protected from draughts and in a steady temperature of about 15°C (60°F).

Other containers

A large shallow bowl or dish can be used to plant a mixture of succulents and cacti. There are hundreds of different types and sizes. The container requires drainage holes or a layer of charcoal in the base with a suitable compost. Place it in good light where the plants can receive sunlight. Water and feed regularly from spring to autumn but less frequently in winter.

A fish tank can be used to make a terrarium for growing tender plants in a humid atmosphere free from draughts. Layer the base with fine gravel and charcoal, and fill with damp compost. Small rocks and pebbles can provide a hilly terrain. A sheet of rigid plastic placed on top of the tank will keep the atmosphere humid. Water very sparingly as the system will recirculate the moisture. Keep it away from direct sunlight. Plant small varieties that are suitable for a terrarium, such as *Acorus*, maidenhair ferns, *Maranta* (prayer plant) and *Selaginella* (Irish moss).

Further reading

Hessayon, D.G. (1995) *The Container Expert.* London: Transworld.

Hessayon, D.G. (1998) *The House Plant Expert.* London: Transworld.

Hessayon, D.G. (1999) *The Flower Expert.* London: Transworld.

See also other books in the Expert gardening series.

Resources

Thrive
The Geoffrey Udall Centre
Beech Hill
Reading
RG7 2AT
Tel: 0119 988 5688
www.thrive.org.uk
A horticultural charity that promotes gardening for people with disabilities and the elderly. It publishes information, leaflets, books on gardening activities.

Peta (UK) Ltd
Marks Hall
Marks Hall Lane
Margaret Roding
Dunmow
Essex
CM6 1QT
Tel: 01215 231811
A supplier of garden tools for older people and those with disabilities.

18

Cookery

For many people, lifelong habits often retain their appeal. The wish to continue to have a hand in cooking is frequently mentioned by residents. There are obviously issues concerning the risks involved, the arrangements necessary and the observance of food hygiene regulations. Yet, with careful forethought and planning it is possible to run a group that takes part in regular cooking sessions.

While it would be ideal to produce a wide range of different foods, it is best not to try to take over the cooking of main meals provided by kitchen staff. The most accessible and enjoyable branch of cookery for a group is the production of cakes, biscuits and pastries. The range of possibilities is very wide and covers recipes from the simplest to the most complex. The results can provide the residents with popular additions to the menu and supply the foundation of that most social of activities: the tea party.

Another good reason for suggesting baking as an activity is to revive it as one of the staples of home cooking it once was. The simple skills of providing home-made cakes and biscuits have been largely replaced in recent times with ready-made supermarket products. These tend to be of indifferent quality compared with home-made items and are usually more costly. However, there are still regions where traditional skills linger, and in small shops, markets and homes can be found such delights as parkin, oatcakes, Scottish shortbreads, Eccles cakes, lardy cake, bannocks and many others.

Apart from members' personal know-how of local favourites and specialities, there is an extensive selection of recipes available in cookery books that cover different regions and other countries around the world. If any members in the group are from other cultural backgrounds they may be able to suggest interesting favourites from abroad.

Planning

Essential precautions are necessary. Keep the group – or groups – small: 4–5 members in a group are sufficient. Close cooperation with the kitchen staff is vital for making suitable arrangements and to ensure safety regulations are observed at all times. Some homes have additional cooking facilities in a suitable room or an area that avoids the use of the main kitchen; and this makes the activity easier to manage.

Equipment

A range of basic utensils and simple equipment is best obtained and kept for the sole use of the group. Store cupboards will be needed for these and for keeping essential ingredients. Hygienic conditions, cleanliness, and personal hygiene by everyone involved must be established and observed at all times.

As well as necessary kitchen utensils for preparing and mixing ingredients, include such items as:

- non-stick cake tins 7 inch (18 cm) and 8 inch (29 cm)

- sandwich tins, baking trays and loaf tins
- non-stick patty tins
- silicon baking paper, paper cake cases
- pastry cutters
- electric hand whisk.

Ingredients

A supply of fresh dairy produce will need to be kept in a refrigerator. In addition, have supplies of:

- different kinds of flour and sugar
- dried fruits, nuts and spices
- baker's chocolate or plain unsweetened chocolate
- baking powder and dried yeast
- golden syrup and honey.

Making a start

- Begin with simple, familiar cakes.
- Use and keep to a reliable recipe.
- Explain clearly how the work will be done.
- Allocate the sharing of tasks and make sure that everyone has something to do, and that they follow instructions.
- Do not be in a hurry. It may cause confusion.

In the early stages, it is important to establish a sound working routine that ensures good results. In time, as confidence and success develop, there will be opportunities for flexibility and the organising of more advanced recipes.

The details that follow do not include recipes. Instead, the most popular categories are given from which choices can be made. Provide recipes for particular items from more than one source so that the kind that is preferred can be chosen.

Categories of cakes

In the following list of main categories, many variations will be possible and will appear in different recipes under different names that are too many to list.

Small, individual cakes

These are the familiar home-made cakes that were baked widely in the past, and which are just as irresistible today. Many have traditional versions associated with a particular region or town, and include:

- fairy cakes
- butterfly cakes
- rock cakes
- oatcakes
- flapjacks
- Welsh cakes
- Eccles cakes
- gingerbread
- brownies.

Large cakes

- Dundee
- fruit cakes
- Madeira
- chocolate
- date and walnut
- ginger
- cherry
- Battenburg
- simnel
- Christmas.

Sponge cakes

- Victoria
- whisked
- Genoese
- Swiss roll
- layered cakes with various flavours and fillings.

Recipes for all these cakes and their many variations are easily found in the many excellent cookery books available today. Some are listed at the end of the chapter.

Problems with cakes

There are bound to be problems and failures at times. Discovering the cause and putting it right is an important part of the activity. There are many different reasons for cakes to fail, too many to list here. Some of the most common are:

- Mixing ingredients – creaming together butter, sugar and eggs should incorporate as much air as possible – using an electric mixer will usually achieve the right balance. Beat eggs separately and add to the mixture gradually, beating well. Flour needs to be folded into a mixture, not stirred or beaten.

- Cake tins – use the size and depth given in the recipe. Grease and line tins with silicon or greaseproof paper.

- Oven temperatures – these can be variable. Check with an oven thermometer.

Categories of biscuits, cookies, pastries and scones

Biscuits are quick to mix and bake. They are far superior to shop-made products and are much cheaper. Make sure that solid baking trays are used that have low or no sides, to allow even baking.

Biscuits and cookies

- shortbreads
- oatmeal cookies
- sesame biscuits
- macaroons
- ginger biscuits
- coconut cookies

- florentines
- cheese biscuits.

Pastries

- Bakewell tart
- almond slices
- chocolate éclairs
- apple strudel
- Black Forest gateau.

Scones and tea breads

- plain and fruit scones
- drop scones
- scone rounds
- Devonshire splits
- muffins
- meringues
- lardy cake
- Bara brith.

Faults to avoid

If biscuits or cookies are too soft the mixture may have been over-creamed, or they may not have been cooked long enough. After cooking allow air to circulate around them.

If too hard, the biscuits have been baked too long or at too high a temperature. If they are too brown there may have been too much greasing of the baking tray – use a pastry brush to spread melted butter.

Oven positions are important. In a gas oven use the top half; in an electric oven use the lower half.

Baking for special occasions and events

- Let members choose their favourites to bake, but check the recipe and the cooking method first.

- Hold a poll among the residents as to the choices they would like.

- Make a calendar of residents' birthdays so that a cake is provided for each of these days.

- Organise tea parties through the year, including outdoor picnics and visits by groups from other care homes.

- Hold some tea dances.

- Have a bring-and-buy sale with biscuits and cakes made in the home to eat and to sell.

- Other anniversaries for a tea party could include New Year's Day, St Valentine's Day, May Day, Mid-summer's Day (24 June), harvest time, Halloween, Guy Fawkes, Christmas.

Sweet making

There are a number of simple but delicious sweets that can be made that need either no cooking or only minimal melting of some ingredients. This avoids the danger of boiling sugar. Recipes for them can be found in some cookery books or in those devoted to making home confectionery. Some sweets that are worth trying are:

- chocolate fudge
- coconut ice
- peppermint creams
- truffles
- uncooked marzipan.

Sweets look attractive when wrapped in clear or coloured cellophane or foil. They can also be stored with or without wrappers in small glass jars that can be decorated with ribbons. However they are presented, they make attractive presents or items for fund-raising events.

Further reading

Maher, B. (1996) *Ultimate Cakes*. London: Dorling Kindersley.

Smith, D. (1987) *Book of Cakes*. London: Guild publishing

Walden, H. (1990) *The Complete Home Confectioner*. London: Ward Lock.

19

Going Out

Taking residents out regularly is less of an activity than an essential part of every person's rights. Throughout life, everyone 'goes out' from home as a matter of course: to school, to work, shopping, to visit friends and relatives, to clubs and pubs, to sports centres, to the library – the list is endless. In old age many people's ability to go out often becomes limited. Physical problems, fewer social contacts, a lack of transport, and safety fears cause them to become homebound and isolated. If they go into a care home things should improve and they should be able to take part in 'going out' again. Unfortunately, in many cases, this does not happen as a regular part of the care. 'Outings' become rare, special occasions that are often much too infrequent.

There are clearly difficulties to overcome, and these are usually used to explain why residents see so little of the outside world. Immobility, disability and a lack of transport are given as the main problems. 'They prefer to stay in', is a commonly expressed reason, but it sounds very much like the result of a long established routine. If outside visits have never been the norm, residents will not expect them.

Local visits

However, some homes make determined efforts to let residents have the freedom of regularly visiting their immediate locality. What is required for this to happen? Committed staff, a team of volunteers, relatives and helpers, and transport are needed. It can be done, because some are doing it. There are care assistants who will enthusiastically push residents in wheelchairs to the local shops, to the park, or to the market or a car boot sale. There can be a mutual advantage – a change of scenery for the staff as well as for their charges.

Nobody should need convincing that regular visits like these in the neighbourhood are worthwhile activities. For the resident they provide a continuing link with their familiar past and local community. The experience is evident on their return. They have something to talk about, things to comment on – their spirits have been lifted.

According to its position, every home will have various local amenities that can be used for short visits:

- shops
- supermarkets
- open markets
- post office
- bank
- church
- café
- library
- pubs
- sports centre
- swimming pool

- bring and buy sales
- school and college events
- shows.

Special visits

Arranging visits to places further afield depends on the position of the home – whether it is in a town, a city or a village. Some rural areas can do nothing without transport. Homes that, through fund-raising or making appeals for contributions in the local community, manage to obtain a minibus or similar vehicle are able to make such outings on a regular basis. In some areas there are organisations that provide community transport which can be used.

Arranging for staff, relatives or volunteers to use their own cars entails checking insurance cover and the suitability of drivers. All these methods are in use in different homes. The results are worth the effort for both the residents who go out and the staff and supporters who make it possible.

Once the matters of transport and enrolling suitable assistants are settled, the choice of places to be visited can be considered. Visits should be chosen according to the number going and the suitability of each person to make the journey and take part in any activity.

Where to go must depend on the interests of the residents:

- museums
- craft fairs, exhibitions
- art displays
- seaside
- rivers, lakes

- zoos, wildlife parks

- concerts

- theatres

- cinemas

- churches, cathedrals, mosques, synagogues.

Other visits

Visits can have other dimensions that have no practical or educational aims. There can be a case for providing experiences that have sensory appeal and through their imagery stimulate the imagination. We are all subject to the effects of the environment. It is possible to draw attention to these matters with short outings for a few interested residents:

- On a fine evening, go to a high point or a wide panorama and watch the sun setting.

- On a fine autumn evening go to watch the rising moon and the first stars.

- Go to high ground above a town after dark and see the patchwork of lights below in the streets and moving traffic.

- Make visits to farms to see ploughing, lambing, harvesting and so on.

- Visit a fairground after dark. Look at the whirling medley of lights and listen to the wild music.

- If you are near a rocky coast, visit on a stormy day and watch the angry waves.

- Visit a lake, a reservoir or a river to watch the wildlife, the water birds, the reflections of trees and clouds.

20

Activities for People with Dementia

Many care homes have residents suffering from dementia. Some homes offer specialist care for people who have developed the condition; others have residents who have developed it in the home as they have become older. As people live longer, the incidence of dementia increases, even though this is a disability that is not caused by the normal ageing process. The majority of people even in their 80s or 90s never develop dementia. Those who do pose difficult problems for the staff who care for them.

Dementia is a terminal condition caused by various disorders of the brain that result in progressive loss of memory and mental ability. The most common form of dementia is caused by Alzheimer's disease. People who develop dementia lose their sense of time and place and find it increasingly difficult to perform everyday tasks or to look after themselves. The rate of deterioration varies, but the condition may last for up to ten years, before a person dies, usually from other causes.

Dementia care

Care for people with dementia has improved in recent times. People with dementia now in nursing or residential homes would once have been incarcerated in an asylum or a geriatric hospital, most of which are now closed. However, dementia care in many homes still leaves a lot to be desired. It requires highly motivated staff who are flexible, responsive and imaginative in developing the therapies the condition demands. Most of the daily hands-on work with such residents is done by care assistants. They are often inexperienced with no formal training of any sort, and may never have attended courses or studied recent books on the subject of dementia. They have usually received in-house training by senior nursing staff or management and been given advice on how to 'manage' residents with dementia, but know little or nothing of the psychological aspects of the condition.

It is to the credit of many care assistants that in time they learn to develop strategies, skills and warm relationships with people with dementia who need their support and understanding. Staff who do this difficult work deserve to receive proper training in dementia care, as well as recognition and better rewards for their commitment to this area of health care.

More needs to be known in care homes of the new dementia care culture that has developed through the work of Tom Kitwood and the Bradford Dementia Group. This aims to improve the well-being of people with dementia through care and activities that focus on the uniqueness of each person and that meet their emotional as well as physical needs. For more information on this technique refer to the book list at the end of the chapter.

The stages of dementia

In the early stages of dementia, a person will usually be able to take part in many activities that are suitable for residents without cognitive impairment. However, most people with dementia who are admitted to care homes are no longer in the early stages and have usually been looked after at home until the carer finds the task beyond them. Among the many disabilities of advanced dementia there is likely to be an inability to communicate clearly, and difficulty in thinking, understanding and learning. There may be constant restlessness, anxiety, fear and outbursts of aggression. The behaviour of a person with dementia, however difficult or disruptive, probably has meaning for the person and may be an outcome of frustration at being unable to communicate or relate to the world and people around.

Each person with dementia is affected by a complex network of different effects. There is a need for a detailed personal assessment and a summary of the things a person can do rather than a list of disabilities. It is important to know first what the person was like before dementia developed.

Knowing the real person

Although a person with dementia behaves differently from the way they did in the past, the real individual still exists. It may be possible to identify the real person if we know as much as possible about them. As well as information from a care plan profile, it is helpful to talk to relatives and friends about the person's background, work, special interests and personality. If the family are willing, collect photographs, letters, cards or any other items that help to build up a life history. This can be the basis of a continuous project with the resident in which contributions are collected over time and put in a loose-leaf binder. A resident's fading memory may make the work halting and irregular, but it is a meaningful therapy and a useful resource for impromptu chats and reminiscences.

The need for special activities

The range of disabilities people with advanced dementia may suffer from often defeats attempts by staff to provide them with suitable activities. The result is that many spend their days doing nothing, sleeping or wandering. Whatever difficulties they may pose, they have the same rights as other people, and should be included in a programme of special activities.

There is a fundamental need to engage them in activities that are on a completely different level to people who have no severe mental disabilities. There should be no attempt to involve them in anything competitive or that requires comprehension, judgement or physical skills. They have an easily aroused sense of failure, and if this occurs it can result in increased anxiety and fear. The frequent lack of communication means that non-verbal alternatives need to be found and these can be best made through sensory approaches. The person with dementia who retains sight, hearing, touch, taste and smell has lines of communication. These can be used by providing activities that have a sensory basis.

The value of any activity for a person with dementia is the actual experience of doing it. For them, there is no yesterday or tomorrow: only now. Take them for a walk. Hold their hand or support their arm. Don't tell them where you are going or why. It will mean nothing to them. Point to the things they can see: the trees, the flowers, the birds, the sky, the clouds. Get them to listen to the things they can hear: the traffic, a distant train, dogs barking, the cries of crows or gulls, insects, the sound of the wind, a plane passing overhead. Help them to feel things they can touch or smell: the grass, the bark of a tree, the shape of acorns or conkers or leaves, a gate post, sand shells, seaweed... Any response? Perhaps, perhaps not. Repeat the process another time. Never give up.

There is a theory that late dementia results in a regression to the level of childhood reasoning and perceptions. Thus, while a child increases in mental development, a person with dementia decreases to the earlier stages they once went though. This should not encourage approaches that are infantile or demeaning. Instead, it should be recognised that the person is still an adult with adult experiences but may now be seeing and experiencing the world with the freedom and perception of a child. The criteria for providing suitable activities that have the appeal of such basic experiences are whether the person gets enjoyment and improved well-being from doing them.

Here are some simple principles that have been found to help in working with people in the later stages of dementia:

- Help the person to trust you and feel safe.

- Appropriate physical contact often helps.

- Use direct eye contact – and smile.

- Speak slowly and quietly; try close-up whispering.

- Never speak 'down' as if the person is a child.

- Go one step at a time.

Activities with sensory applications

These suggestions are for people with late or advanced dementia and who have limited abilities and diminishing awareness of the people and events around them. They may be done on a one-to-one basis or with small groups.

The sessions will be helped with the active – and enthusiastic – involvement of an assistant, or carer or relative who is prepared to enter into the spirit of the activity. Keep each session short. Aim to provide enjoyment, pleasure and good humour. Laughter can often be infectious even to people with dementia. It's what most of them need.

Music

Make a collection of a wide variety of recorded music, songs, chants, hymns and carols. What music evokes memories for you? Nursery rhymes, street rhymes, ball games, films, musicals, television, discos? People in their 70s or 80s today may have memories of music that goes back to the 1930s or before. Try to ignore the archaic Victorian music hall songs that have become synonymous with elderly people's singalongs. Play them some Judy Garland, songs by Cole Porter, Jerome Kern, Vera Lynn, the Beatles, Abba and many more from the recent past. Have some lively marches, waltzes and country dance music.

Get them singing or accompanying the music with their hands or percussion instruments. Invite, encourage and cajole them to dance. Some will, some won't, but they may enjoy watching. In later sessions more may join in.

Here are two verses of an invitation to dance from *Hansel and Gretel*:

> Brother come and dance with me;
> Both my hands I offer thee,
> Right foot first,
> Left foot then,
> Round about and back again.

With your foot you tap tap tap
With your hand you clap clap clap
Right foot first
Left foot then,
Round about and back again.

(See also Chapter 13 on music.)

Poetry and verse

It was mentioned earlier that a person with advanced dementia may be experiencing a return to the perceptions of childhood. Whether this is true or not, poetry and verse can be an enjoyable and interesting activity to use. It can provide simple and imaginative ideas and striking pictures, and only demands careful choice and an enthusiastic reader.

What sort of poetry? Avoid nursery rhymes intended for the very young, even though some of these may bring back memories to some. Choose poems that are suitable for the 10–15-year-old range. Some of the best poems for the young are just as suitable for any age to read – including you. A poem can jog a memory, convey a simple truth, illuminate beauty, evoke curiosity or amusement. And this makes many poems suitable for a person with dementia to hear. Look at these verses from a poem written for children by Eleanor Farjeon:[1]

It Was Long Ago

I'll tell you, shall I, something I remember?
Something that still means a great deal to me.
It was long ago.

A dusty road in summer I remember,
A mountain and an old house, and a tree
That stood, you know

Behind the house. An old woman I remember
In a red shawl with a grey cat on her knee
Humming under a tree.

And while she hummed, and the cat purred,
I remember
How she filled a saucer with berries and cream
for me
So long ago.

There are many anthologies of poetry for the young and the developing young that have poems and verse suitable for reading on a one-to-one basis or to a small group. If you enjoy a poem, so probably will your listeners when you read it to them. Some suggested titles that may be in a local library are listed at the end of the chapter.

(See the section on poetry in Chapter 15, page 97.)

Other activities

- Games – simple games with soft balls, balloons and bubbles.

- Aromatherapy and massage. Both are best done by a practitioner or someone who has had experience and training in their application.

- Rummaging – make collections in boxes or bags of objects that are safe to examine, explore and touch that may remind a person of other times – keys, a glove, a purse, a torch, a clock, a watch, a necklace, a piece of driftwood, silk, linen, fur, a magnifying glass, a doll, a soft toy.

- Scrapbooks – containing large pictures from magazines, colour supplements, travel brochures and local photographs of scenes and people.

- Multisensory room or Snoezelen: a combination of lighting effects, soothing music or sounds, attractive scents, different materials to touch. An alternative is a 'white room' – walls and furnishing in soft shades of white with subdued lighting and quiet background music.

- Regular short outings to provide a change of scene and to experience different surroundings.

- Reminiscence – depends of the stage of dementia a person has reached. See Chapter 11 on reminiscence.

Note

1. Farjeon, E. (1999) 'It Was Long Ago.' From *Blackbird Has Spoken:* Basingstoke: Macmillan.

Further reading

Benson, S. and Kitwood, T. (eds) (1995) *The New Culture of Dementia Care, Bradford Dementia Group.* London: Hawker Publications.

Causley, C. (2000) *Collected Poems for Children.* Basingstoke: Macmillan Children's Books.

Foster, J. (2000) *First Oxford Book of Poems.* Oxford: Oxford University Press. (Traditional to modern.)

Harrison, M. and Stuart-Clark, C. (1991) *A Year Full of Poems.* Oxford: Oxford University Press.

Kitwood, T. (1997) *Dementia Reconsidered.* Buckingham: Open University Press.

Perrin, R.T. and May, H. (1999) *Wellbeing in Dementia.* London: Churchill Livingstone.

Rosen, M. (1985) *The Kingfisher Book of Children's Poetry.* Basingstoke: Kingfisher Books.